Whilst writing this book the author has tried to e[...] in this guide is up to date and accurate before p[...] medical information is constantly being updated as new researc[...] t and guidelines change. Therefore please ensure you consult a qualified healthcare professional before considering any changes to your lifestyle. The knowledge and advice provided in this book are based on the research and the personal and professional experiences of the author. They are not intended as a substitute for consulting with a healthcare professional. The publisher and author are not responsible for any adverse effects or consequences resulting from the use of any of the suggestions, preparations, or procedures discussed in this book. Never stop taking any prescribed medication unless you have been advised by medical staff. All matters about your physical health should be supervised by a healthcare professional.

The target reference ranges for glucose, cholesterol, blood pressure, kidney function, weight and urine microalbumin levels and any other tests/parameters/diagnostic levels mentioned are as per UK recommended guidance. If you are a non UK resident please check with your healthcare professionals what your standard ranges should be as this may vary for each country.

Author: Kavita Sharma
Cover Design: Kavita Sharma via Canva & AI generated
Illustrations: Canva & as per references
Photography for Recipes: Kavita Sharma
Self Published
Published in UK 2023

ISBN 978-1-7395016-0-0

The Desi Diabetes Guide

@desidiabetes

desidiabetesuk

desidiabetes.co.uk

TABLE OF CONTENTS

01

INTRODUCTION

THE DESI DIABETES GUIDE

This book is dedicated to my wonderful, amazing parents. My mum was not given a chance to further her education but has lived her dream of education through her four children. Her loving nature has taught me to help others whilst always being proud of my South Asian heritage. While growing up my dad always instilled the importance of knowledge and health, even now he still researches health topics, to provide everyone with tips. The combination of both of their values has inspired me to write this book to help improve the lives and health of others. Thank you both for your love and guidance, without your upbringing, I would not be where I am today.

It was whilst I was pregnant with my beautiful daughter that I was inspired to create the concept of Desi Diabetes and write this book, so thank you Shivani for also being my inner voice and inspiration. I would like to thank my husband, Deeraj for supporting me during this venture, even when he thought it was another of my crazy ideas! And a massive thank you to all my lovely family and friends for supporting me and giving me advice and ideas. A special thanks to my siblings especially my sisters, brother and bhabi, who have supported me so much over the last year, from helping me with social media to always being proud of my small achievements. Thanks to my mother in law for coming along to my classes and helping me set up. Also a special thanks to Professor Vinod Patel for his knowledge and guidance. Thank you to everyone for always supporting what I do and most importantly helping me to spread the word about healthy living. Together I hope we can help create a healthier future for the next generation.

I have written this book whilst on my maternity leave, it's amazing what you can achieve as a mother. I had no prior experience in starting a business, setting up a website, or writing a book. I have managed to learn all this as well as create this entire book from writing to publishing, all completed during my maternity leave. So for all the mums out there – keep doing what you are doing, you are truly capable of amazing things!

INTRODUCTION

Health should be equal for all

South Asians are six times more likely to develop Diabetes than European populations [1]; despite this, there isn't enough accessible Diabetes information available for people of this community. This book, The Desi Diabetes Guide, is a guide targeted at educating South Asians on the key things they need to know about Diabetes so that we can help prevent this condition and reduce the dangerous complications it often leads to.

As a Pharmacist with over 12 years of experience, including the last six years specialising in Diabetes as a Clinical Pharmacist, I've always been passionate about this field. During my time in a GP surgery, I noticed a significant gap: insufficient educational resources for educating the South Asian population about Diabetes and healthy living. Often, patients receive a Diabetes diagnosis during a brief 10-minute consultation with their GP. They're prescribed medication and advised to improve their lifestyle. But what about South Asian patients who speak limited English, cook traditional Asian foods, and have never exercised? Where do they begin?

While there are Diabetes educational courses available, they're typically conducted in English, centralised in city locations, and focused on a Western diet. For our South Asian patients, these barriers create health inequalities. Many lack transportation options, making it challenging to attend these courses.

Over time, these patients may require multiple medications for their Diabetes, experiencing complications earlier than other ethnicities. The root cause lies in their limited understanding of Diabetes. Without comprehension, effective management becomes difficult. To address these disparities, I created the Desi Diabetes Guide - a culturally sensitive resource. Additionally, my company, Desi Diabetes, offers Punjabi-language classes on Diabetes and healthy living within local communities. This way, we can empower our community with enough knowledge to allow them to make better lifestyle choices to improve their health.

The name 'Desi Diabetes' was chosen to resonate with those from South Asian backgrounds, as 'Desi' often refers to individuals from Indian, Pakistani, and Bangladeshi heritage. Additionally, 'Desi' carries connotations of purity. Personally, I've always appreciated the traditional roots of living, and adopting a health-conscious lifestyle with wholesome foods can significantly reduce our risk of Diabetes.

When it comes to the initial diagnosis of Type 2 Diabetes, I firmly believe that what caused it could potentially cure it. If poor diet and lifestyle choices contributed to the condition, then adopting a healthier, more active lifestyle could be part of the solution. This message is central to my book. Returning to basics, we must educate patients about the different food groups and their effects on our bodies. Discussing healthy swaps and finding ways to continue enjoying South Asian cuisine in a more health-conscious manner should be our focus. Rather than asking patients to completely abandon the foods they know how to cook, we should empower them to make these meals healthier by adjusting ingredients and cooking methods. While various diet plans exist, from low-calorie meal replacements to no-carbohydrate diets, we must consider what happens after the initial three months. What lasting knowledge have individuals gained about their dietary choices?

To address these challenges, our approach to preventing Type 2 Diabetes and its complications should emphasize culturally tailored diet education. We need a paradigm shift in healthcare delivery—one that enables patients to make informed lifestyle decisions not only for their own future but also for the well-being of their families. My goal is to re-educate our community about Diabetes, healthy eating, and overall well-being, empowering them to lead healthier, happier lives.

Desi Diabetes was launched earlier this year, and as part of this, I have held numerous classes hosted in Punjabi for diabetes prevention in the form of diet and exercise programmes. This has resulted in people making healthier diet choices, learning about new foods, socialising with one another, getting involved and enjoying exercise. There have also been some great results with weight loss.

In this book, we will discuss what Diabetes is, what causes it, and the complications that could arise. I will also discuss how we can improve our lifestyle to prevent Diabetes and reverse it. I have included some healthy South Asian recipes for you to try so that you can learn to cook more nutritious foods but still enjoy those great flavours.

02

TYPE 2 DIABETES

As with all medication, it has been prescribed for a reason so do not stop any of your medicines unless advised by your GP. Please consult with your healthcare team before considering any lifestyle changes. If after making changes to your lifestyle your glucose levels change, your GP will advise you whether any changes to your medication are needed, but never stop taking your medication yourself. If you are on Insulin or on a Sulfonylurea medication such as Gliclazide, Glipizide, Glimepiride, or Tolbutamide which can cause hypoglycaemia, please speak to your healthcare professional before making any dietary or lifestyle changes.

TYPES OF DIABETES

There are two common types of Diabetes, Type 1 and Type 2.

Type 1 Diabetes

Type 1 Diabetes is a severe condition as the body stops making Insulin altogether. This results in raised glucose levels that can be life-threatening. It is thought to occur due to the body attacking the pancreatic cells that produce Insulin, which usually develops in childhood. It is not linked to lifestyle, it is not preventable, it cannot be reversed, and it must be treated with lifelong Insulin.

Type 2 Diabetes

Type 2 Diabetes is usually lifestyle-related, linked to genetics, diet and lack of physical activity. It tends to develop gradually over time, usually in adulthood, but it is preventable and reversible.

In this book, we will be focusing on Type 2 Diabetes.

DIABETES AND LIFESTYLE

In 1980 there were an estimated **108 million** people in the world with diabetes. In 2014, this trebled to **422 million** people [2]. After nine years, the cases are estimated to be even higher today. In addition to this, in 2019, there was an estimated **Two million deaths** due to Diabetes [2].

Recently it has come to light that there are more than **100 million cases of Diabetes in India** alone, accompanied by **136 million cases of Pre-Diabetes**, both thought to be attributed to diets high in sugary and fatty foods and low physical activity [27]. It seems as though the lifestyle we adapted to in the West has also found its way back home.

Let's reflect on how our lives have evolved from the 1980s to today. While the world has made rapid progress, our lifestyle choices have taken a toll on our health, leading to numerous health conditions. Did people in the 1980s have the same awareness about Diabetes as we do now? Today, knowledge is at our fingertips - thanks to mobile devices and the internet. Gone are the days of visiting libraries for research; now, we can access information instantly. However, there's a paradox: despite our increased awareness, we often fail to make substantial lifestyle improvements. Our elders, living in our native homelands, consumed similar desi foods (albeit purer versions) without developing Diabetes. Why? Firstly, the diagnostic testing available today didn't exist in their time. Secondly, our grandparents led more active lives. Picture their mornings: a hearty breakfast of paratha with makhan (clarified butter), full-fat yogurt, and a glass of full-fat milk. Men would head out on foot to work manually in the fields, while women prepared fresh meals at home - grinding flour using a chakki, milking cows, churning butter by hand, blending saag, and handwashing clothes.

Now contrast this with our modern lives. Many of these traditional foods come pre-packaged, even down to ready-made parathas and sabzis. Our challenge lies in bridging the gap between our ancestors' active lifestyles and our convenience-driven routines. Perhaps it's time to revisit our roots, embrace healthier choices, and strike a balance between tradition and modernity.

In our modern lives, convenience has become our ally and our adversary. We drive everywhere, spend hours at office desks, and rely on machines to wash our clothes - even the act of hanging laundry has been replaced by the convenience of dryers. At night, we don't need to get out of bed to turn off the lights; Alexa handles it for us. She'll even boil our kettle! But amidst this convenience, our physical activity levels have plummeted, and our diets have shifted toward processed foods with larger portion sizes. Unfortunately, these changes take a toll on our health.

Consider our energy balance: the calories we consume often exceed what we burn, leading to weight gain. And cooking? Well, that's a few taps away on our mobiles, no need to leave the sofa and a cooked meal of our choice will be delivered to our front door. Our hands and fingers seem to be our most active body parts these days.

Now, let's rewind to the past. Basic household chores, like scrubbing floors (charoo & pocha) in our homes - doubled as workouts. Squatting to clean strengthened leg and pelvic muscles. Women cooked in this position too, as the chula (outdoor cooking fire) was located on the floor. This squatting stance, known as the Malasana position, likely contributed to the good reproductive health of South Asian women.

But as technology advanced, these little exercises dwindled, along with their health benefits. Today, larger portions of processed foods and sedentary lifestyles contribute to preventable lifestyle illnesses. Billions are spent on treating conditions like Type 2 Diabetes, yet prevention efforts remain inadequate. Consequently, the number of people diagnosed with Type 2 Diabetes or Pre-Diabetes continues to rise, along with complications and mortality related to this condition.

UNDERSTANDING TYPE 2 DIABETES

In Punjabi, we often call Diabetes – Sugar di bamari, which translates to a disease of sugar. Due to this, many people believe it is only caused by sugary foods, but it is more complex than that. To fully understand Diabetes, we need to understand the role of Insulin.

Here is an illustration to explain the relationship between carbohydrates, glucose and Insulin.

Insulin is a hormone that is produced by the cells in the pancreas

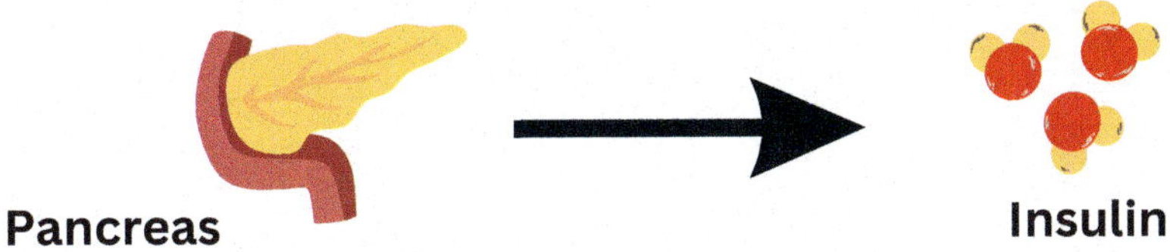

Carbohydrates and any sugary foods we eat are converted into glucose once digested.

When blood glucose levels rise, the pancreas secretes Insulin in response to the glucose

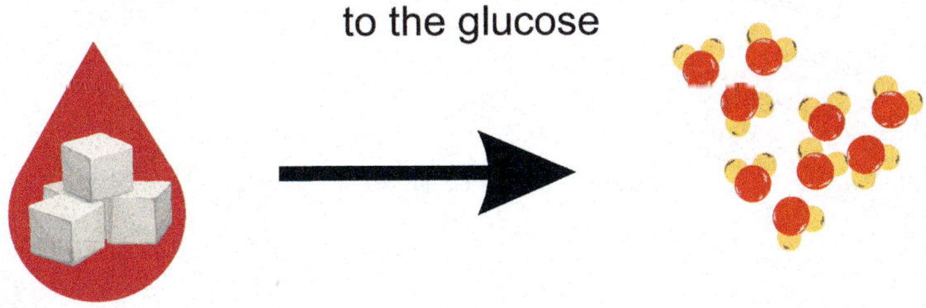

This allows the cells to convert glucose into energy

During Type 2 Diabetes, the body either reduces the amount of Insulin it produces, or Insulin resistance develops. When glucose levels rise frequently, Insulin is produced repeatedly, but over time, our body's response to Insulin reduces; this is Insulin resistance. If you think about using a machine constantly, it eventually loses its effect. This is similar to what happens during Insulin resistance, the repeated intake of carbohydrates/glucose causes the constant release of Insulin, and ultimately, the effect of Insulin begins to wear off. Due to the body's response to Insulin declining, less glucose is removed from the blood, and because of this, glucose begins to accumulate in the blood leading to Type 2 Diabetes.

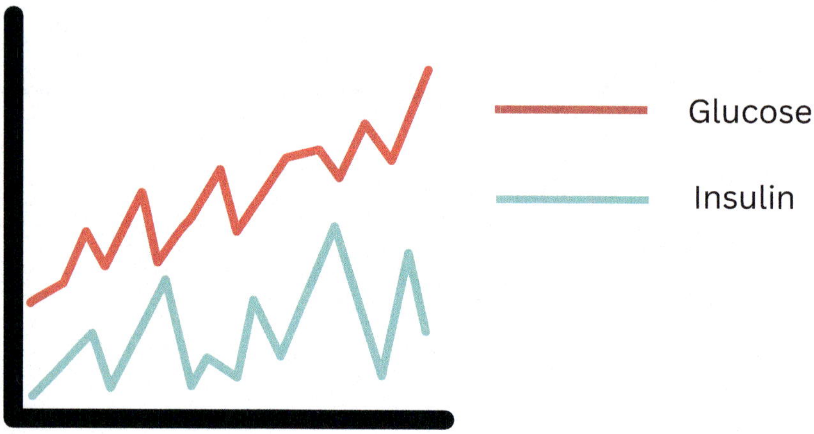

When glucose accumulates in the blood, the liver and muscles store excess glucose in the form of Glycogen. Later when the body needs extra glucose, Glucagon is released by the pancreas, which converts Glycogen back into glucose. When Glycogen's muscles and liver stores get full, the excess glucose is converted into fat and stored in the body for energy for later use.

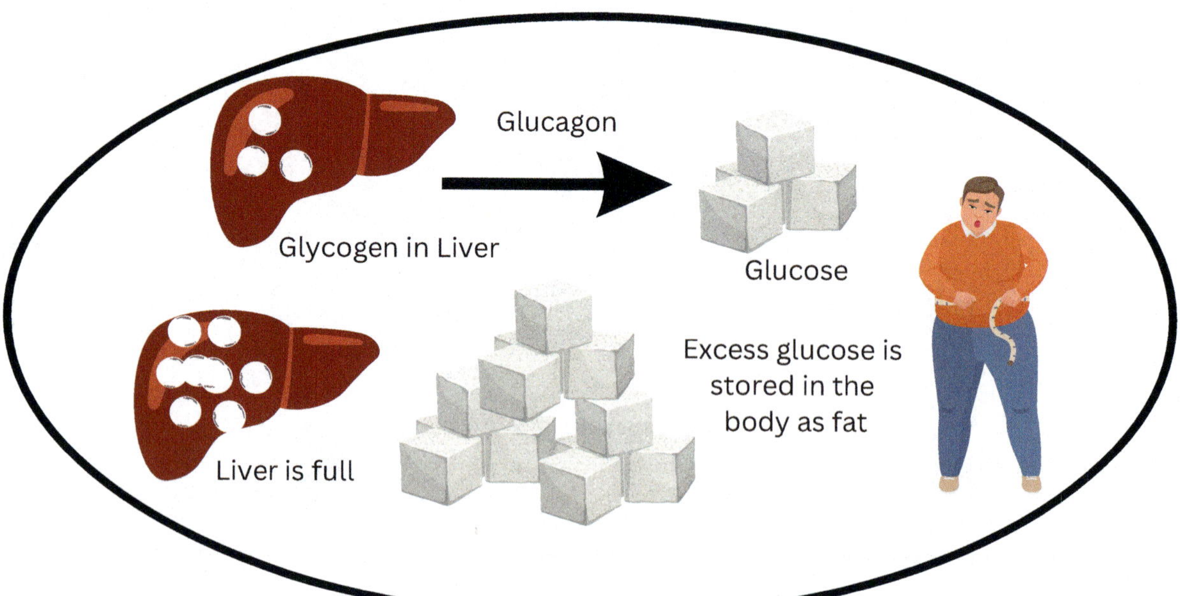

WHAT CAUSES TYPE 2 DIABETES?

Many factors are associated with developing Type 2 Diabetes. Here are some of the common risk factors:

- **A Family history of Diabetes** - Due to genetics as well as following the same diet/lifestyle as our family
- **Belonging to a South Asian background** - Being South Asian, you are six times more likely to develop Diabetes in comparison to Europeans [1], again linked to diet and genetics
- **Being overweight or obese** - Due to the distribution of fat and glucose in the body, Insulin sensitivity is reduced. South Asians have a lower threshold of a BMI over 23 for increased risk of Diabetes in comparison to other populations
- **Having a large waist size** – It is thought that fat around the waist area coats the organs in that area, preventing them from working efficiently. A waist size of more than 80cm is a high risk for women. For South Asian men, a waist size of more than 90cm is high risk. (As a general rule, your waist should be half or less than your height measurement)
- **Having an inactive lifestyle** – Glucose begins to accumulate as it's not utilised by the cells for energy
- **A history of Gestational Diabetes** – If you had Diabetes during pregnancy, you should continue to have a yearly blood test to monitor your glucose levels. (This will be a routine blood test and will not involve the sugary drink you consumed during pregnancy).
- **Taking certain medications** - Such as long-term steroid tablets, could also increase glucose levels
- **Being over the age of 25** - South Asians are at a greater risk of Type 2 Diabetes from the age of 25 compared to Europeans carrying this risk after age 40.

[28]

SYMPTOMS OF DIABETES

How the body reacts to high glucose levels gives rise to each of these symptoms. If you are Diabetic and experiencing any of these symptoms, it may indicate your Diabetes is poorly controlled, and it would be wise to have a blood test done to determine your glucose levels. If you do not have Diabetes but are experiencing any of these symptoms, please speak to your GP to request a glucose blood test to rule out Diabetes.

Tiredness
due to the body not being able to use glucose to produce enough energy

Toilet
urinating more than usual as the body tries to expel excess glucose through urine

Thirst
needing to replace fluid due to urinating frequently

Thinner
body begins to use fat for energy instead of glucose

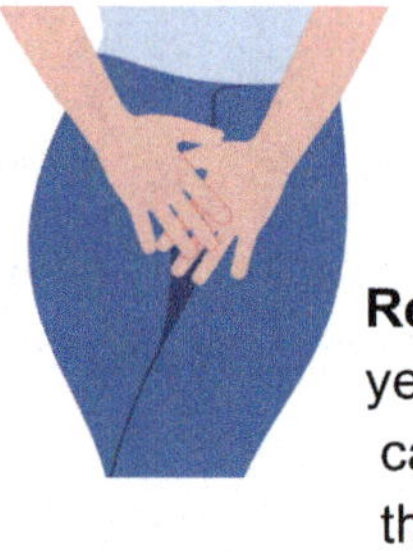

Recurrent thrush
yeast infections are more likely as candida grow in this environment where there's more glucose

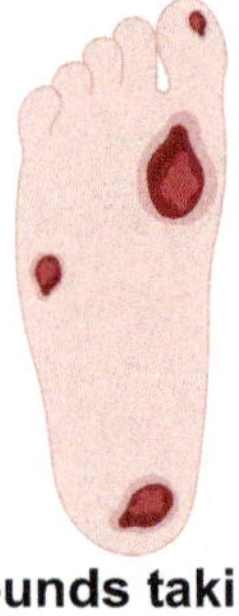

Cuts/wounds taking longer to heal
due to circulation problems

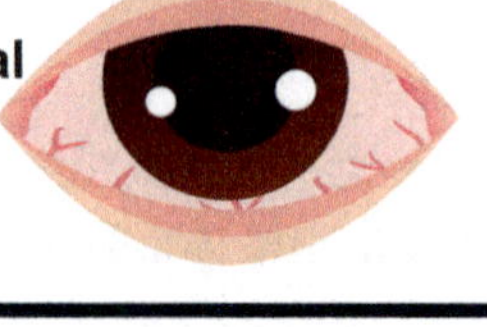

Blurred vision
may be early retinopathy

DIAGNOSIS OF DIABETES

Here in the UK, Diabetes is classed as having an **Hba1c of more than 48mmol/mol** or a **fasting serum glucose of more than 7mmol/l** accompanied by symptoms of Diabetes [3], as mentioned on the previous page. If, however, your glucose levels are high, but you do not have any symptoms of Diabetes, then your GP should repeat your glucose blood test to determine whether you have Type 2 Diabetes. If the second blood test also shows high glucose levels, you will likely be treated as having Type 2 Diabetes.

GLUCOSE BLOOD TESTS

There are two standard blood glucose tests, fasting serum glucose and Hba1c.
Fasting serum glucose tells us your glucose levels at the point the blood sample is taken. This is affected by food and drinks, and to gain a reliable result, it must be done fasting, usually at least 8 hours without food or drink, except water. The **Hba1c** blood test tells us how much glucose has been attached to our red blood cells over the last three months; this reading is more accurate as it gives us a better average of glucose levels.

PRE DIABETES

If your **Hba1c is between 42- 47mmol/mol** or you have a **fasting serum glucose of 5.5- 6.9mmol/l**,[4] your healthcare team may have told you are 'Pre-Diabetic'. This does not mean you have Diabetes, but your glucose levels are at the higher end of normal, which means you have a greater risk of developing Diabetes in the future. At this point, you should start to change your lifestyle and diet to reduce your blood glucose levels to prevent you from developing Diabetes. Your healthcare professional will usually ask you to repeat your glucose blood test in a year to ensure your levels are controlled. However, if you have any symptoms of Diabetes, then please get in contact with your medical team to have that blood test done sooner.
Later in the book, you can learn about the lifestyle changes that will help prevent you from developing Diabetes. **Through lifestyle changes, Pre Diabetes can be reversed**.

REVERSIBILITY

A while ago Type 2 Diabetes was considered a progressive condition with no turning back. However, recent studies have revealed a different story: Type 2 Diabetes can be reversed. A diagnosis of Type 2 Diabetes or Pre-Diabetes doesn't necessarily mean a lifelong sentence. When you receive an initial diagnosis, your healthcare provider typically allows three months for lifestyle changes before considering medication (based on your blood glucose levels). If you commit to making healthy adjustments to your diet, exercise routine, and, if necessary, weight loss, you can potentially reverse Diabetes and restore your glucose levels to normal. This phenomenon is known as diabetes in remission. To qualify, your HbA1c levels must remain below 48 mmol/mol or fasting serum glucose below 7 mmol/L on two separate occasions, with at least a 6-month interval [5].

Should your Diabetes go into remission, it's crucial to maintain the lifestyle changes that got you there. Reverting to old habits could elevate your glucose levels once again. Instead, embrace healthy living as a lifelong commitment for your well-being.

Remember, if you're taking any medications, continue following your prescribed regimen. If your glucose levels normalize, your healthcare provider will guide you on any necessary medication adjustments. Never discontinue medications without professional advice. Regular blood tests, recommended by your GP, will help assess whether your lifestyle can sustain remission or if additional measures are needed. At least a yearly blood glucose test will be needed to monitor remission.

Weight loss is one of the key factors in reversing Diabetes so if you are overweight, weight loss is a great place to start. In addition to this healthy eating - stopping consumption of processed foods/drinks, limiting sugar and refined carbohydrates and most importantly increasing regular moderate intensity exercise will all contribute to your steps towards remission.

03

TREATMENT & COMPLICATIONS

LONG TERM COMPLICATIONS OF DIABETES

If glucose levels continue to rise and Diabetes remains uncontrolled this can lead to many life-threatening complications, these include:

Cardiovascular Complications:

Heart attack & Stroke

Strokes and heart attacks tend to happen when the blood vessels leading to these organs become blocked with cholesterol. Our fingers get sticky if we think about touching something sweet, such as a jalebi. In the same way, our vessels become sticky as more glucose sticks to our red blood cells. This damages the vessels and the addition of high cholesterol can further increase the narrowing of the blood vessels leading to clot formation. Both strokes and heart attacks can be life-threatening. Thus, it is essential to maintain good glucose and cholesterol levels to prevent these conditions.

When the vessel leading to the heart becomes blocked oxygen doesn't reach the heart and heart attack occurs

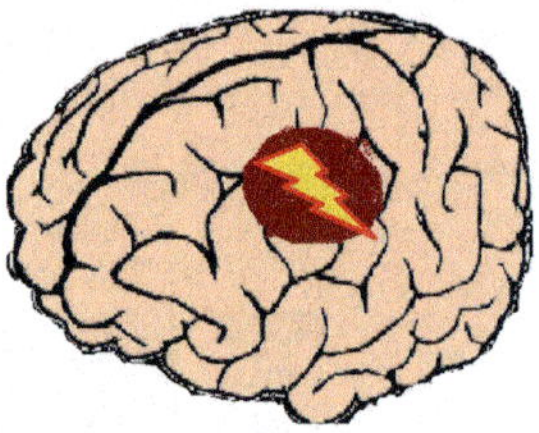

When the vessel leading to the brain becomes blocked oxygen doesn't reach the brain and stroke occurs

Kidney Failure

Diabetic patients are more prone to kidney failure, this risk further increases if you also have high blood pressure. The kidneys help to eliminate waste, excess fluid and help balance the salts in our body but over time, Diabetics can develop small pouches in the kidney vessels which start to leak out protein into the urine.

Initially, this is treated with medication, usually starting with an ACE Inhibitor which is also a blood pressure medication. If medication fails to control the condition then dialysis is started and if this fails to work then a kidney transplant may be needed.

Eye Problems

The tiny blood vessels behind the eyes can become damaged, which can lead to retinopathy – this may cause visual issues and blindness.

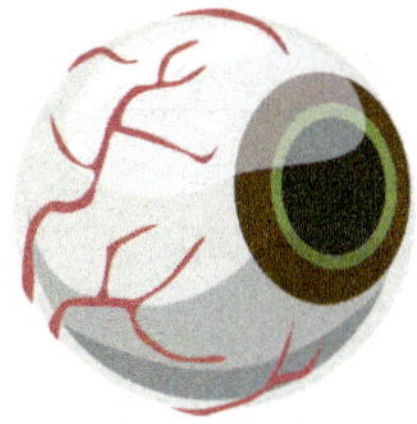

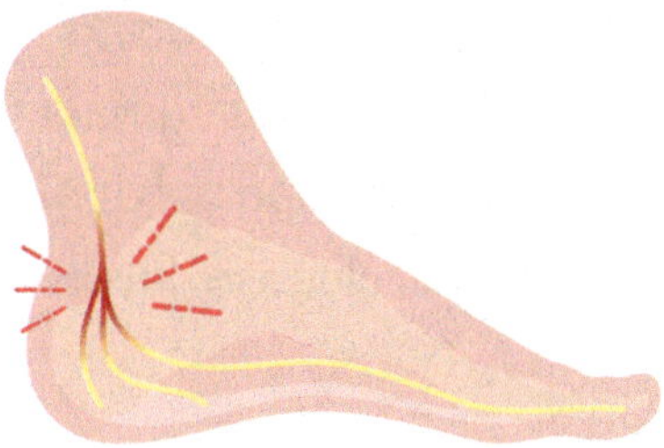

Nerve Damage

Over time, nerve damage can occur which leads to loss of sensation or numbness particularly in the lower limbs.

Foot Infections/Amputations

Gradually the circulation to lower limbs may reduce, in combination with nerve damage, which leads to slower healing of cuts and infections of the feet. If left untreated, the infection can spread, becoming very dangerous and requiring amputation to prevent the infection from spreading. Sometimes it could be a simple toenail not being appropriately cut that causes an infection. If the infection becomes severe and spreads, it may be a toe that needs to be amputated, or part of the foot or part of the leg, depending on how far the infection has spread.

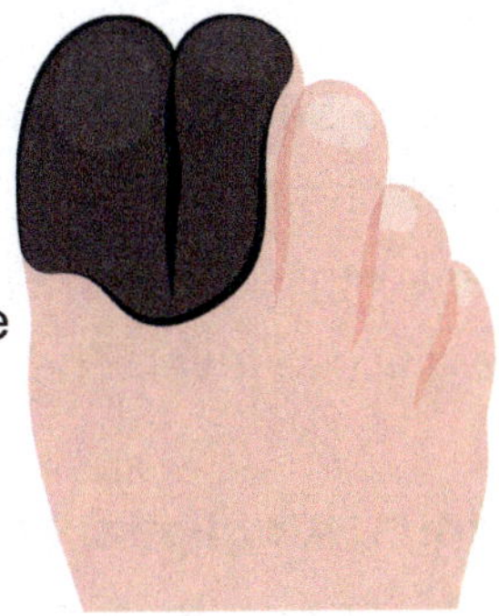

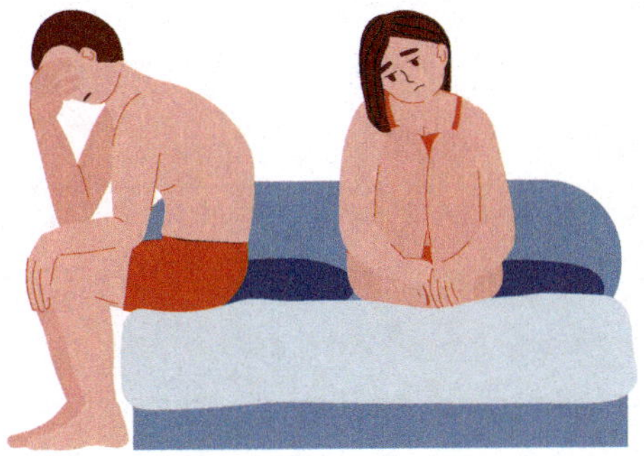

Impotence/ Erectile Dysfunction

High glucose levels can start to affect the blood supply to the penis due to nerve and circulation damage, as a result some men find it difficult to get an erection or to maintain it. This can cause impotence/erectile dysfunction and may effect your sex life.

Treatment To Control Glucose Levels

As a diagnosed Diabetic, your Hba1c levels should be around 48 mmol/l [6]. During an initial diagnosis of Diabetes, your GP will usually allow you three months to make lifestyle changes to improve your glucose levels (dependent on blood glucose levels). If you make effective changes, you will be a diet-controlled diabetic. If glucose levels remain high after making changes to your lifestyle, you will most likely be started on medication. Below is a list of common Diabetes medications prescribed to help lower glucose levels and their mechanism of action.

Metformin

Belongs to the Biguanides family and works by preventing the liver from converting glycogen back into glucose. It also helps to increase the use of glucose in the body by increasing the uptake by muscles thus reducing glucose levels. It's usually taken as an oral tablet.

Gliclazide, Glipizide, Glimepiride, Tolbutamide

These belong to the Sulfonylurea family and work by increasing the amount of Insulin the pancreas makes. This allows more glucose to be converted to energy and as a result lowers glucose level. These are usually taken as an oral tablet.

Sitagliptin, Alogliptin, Linagliptin, Saxagliptin, Vildagliptin

These belong to the DPP4 inhibitor family and work by increasing Insulin secretion and lowering glucagon secretion (prevents glycogen converting back into glucose). These are usually taken as an oral tablet.

Dapagliflozin, Empagliflozin, Canagliflozin, Ertugliflozin

These belong to the SGLT2 inhibitor family, and they work by preventing the kidneys reabsorbing glucose so the excess glucose is removed out through the urine. These are usually taken as an oral tablet.

Pioglitazone

This belongs to the Thiazolidinedione family and work by reducing Insulin resistance so helps to reduce glucose levels. This is usually taken as an oral tablet.

Repaglinide

This belongs to the Meglitinides family and works by increasing Insulin secretion. This is usually taken as an oral tablet.

Acarbose

This belongs to the alpha-glucosidase inhibitors and works by slowing down digestion and absorption of starch and sucrose. This is usually taken as an oral tablet.

Semaglutide, Dulaglutide, Exenatide, Liraglutide, Lixisenatide

These belong to the GLP1 family and work by increasing insulin secretion, prevents glucagon secretion, and slowing gastric emptying thus suppressing appetite. Most often prescribed as an injection but some are available in tablet form

Insulin

Prescribed as injection form or administered using a pump, usually administered as daily injections in the stomach area. Comes as various different types with varying durations of action.

If after an initial diagnosis of Type 2 Diabetes, diet changes fail to control blood glucose levels, and levels remain above an Hba1c of 48mmol/mol, Metformin is usually prescribed as a first line [6]. After at least three months on this medication, you should have a repeated blood test, and if glucose levels remain uncontrolled, then a second medication is added. Again, if glucose levels remain high, a third medication is added.

Under the NHS, a maximum of 3 oral medicines are usually given to control glucose levels [6]. If glucose levels remain uncontrolled on these medicines, a GLP1 injection is generally initiated. If this fails to make any improvements, then Insulin would be the last resort which involves daily injection, usually into the stomach.

Initially, when many newly diagnosed patients are commenced on medication for Diabetes, they think they can continue eating and drinking as they are as the medication will do its work. But as time goes by, the medicine's effectiveness reduces due to our body's Insulin levels also reducing. Often at this stage, Insulin injections are initiated. Hence, we must ensure we are eating healthily and exercising regularly to do the best we can to prevent these complications and prevent the need for these treatments.

MEDICATION FOR DIABETES COMPLICATIONS

Medication To Control Cholesterol

As a Diabetic it is essential to control your Cholesterol levels as you are at a greater risk of cardiovascular diseases such as stroke and heart attacks. A healthy total cholesterol reading should be 5mmol/L or less [7]. But whether Cholesterol-lowering medication is needed will be based on your QRISK score, usually, if it is above 10% medication such as a Statin may be initiated to help lower your cholesterol levels [8]. QRISK gives us an estimated risk of how likely you are to suffer from a heart attack or stroke over the next 10 years.

Medication to Control High Blood Pressure

Due to the high risk of heart attacks, strokes, and kidney complications, it is important to maintain a healthy blood pressure, an ideal target blood pressure reading should be less than 135/85mmHg (home setting) or 140/90mmHg (clinic setting) [9]. If it is persistently higher than this then medication for high blood pressure may be initiated, usually an ACE inhibitor. If blood pressure remains raised, then another medication may be initiated and then again another until adequate blood pressure is achieved.

Medication To Protect the Kidneys

If you are found to have protein-leaking kidneys, then a medication called an ACE inhibitor may be started to help prevent further damage to the kidneys. If this fails to improve kidney function additional medication may need to be prescribed which is usually initiated by a kidney specialist, known as a renal consultant. If medication fails to help then Dialysis may be needed, if this fails to work then a kidney transplant would be the last step.

Medication For Neuropathy

Some Diabetic patients may begin to experience neuropathic pain, the pain of the nerves, or numbness in certain parts of the body particularly the feet. To control these symptoms, you may be started on medication usually Amitriptyline or Gabapentin.

Medication for Erectile Dysfunction

To help this condition, some patients may be prescribed Sildenafil or similar medication.

As you can see over time a Diabetic patient could end up on a cocktail of medicines as the condition progresses and complications begin to arise. If you are on any prescribed medication, never stop taking the medication unless you are advised by your GP as the complications of Diabetes can be extremely dangerous if not controlled.

ACUTE DIABETES COMPLICATIONS

Hypoglycaemia (Hypos)

If serum glucose levels fall below 4mmol/l, we call this hypoglycaemia aka 'hypos'. This is an indication that your sugars have fallen below normal. It may affect those on Insulin or Sulfonylurea medication such as Glimepiride, Gliclazide, Glipizide, or Tolbutamide.

Symptoms of Hypos include:

- Feeling tired
- Sweating
- Confusion
- Palpitations
- Shaking
- Feeling hungry

Treatment

Readings of less than 4mmol/L should be treated straight away by consuming something with a fast-acting carbohydrate, such as:

- 5 glucose or dextrose tablets
- 200ml of pure fruit juice
- Half a can (150ml) of sugary drink (make sure it's not sugar-free)
- 2 glucose gel tubes such as GlucoGel

Check your sugar levels again after treatment, if they remain below 4mmol/l take some more of the above treatment [10]. If your next meal is not due for a while, follow this treatment with a slower-acting carbohydrate such as a banana, glass of milk, or a piece of toast to maintain normal sugar levels. If left untreated hypos can cause seizures, unconsciousness, and hospitalisation.

Driving

For those of you in the UK that are on Insulin or Sulfonylurea, ensure your sugar levels are 5mmol/l or above before you drive. It's especially important to test before starting a long journey and ensure you carry something sweet with you in case of hypos. If you suffer from Hypos or your medical team have advised you are at high risk of hypos then you will need to inform DVLA before you drive. If your are on Insulin and treatment will last over 3 month you will also need to contact the DVLA. [11]

Diabetic Ketoacidosis (DKA)

Although not common this condition can be very severe and requires urgent medical treatment. Some Diabetic medicines can cause Diabetic Ketoacidosis. In Type 1 Diabetes it can happen due to a total lack of Insulin and in Type 2 Diabetes it is due to a severe Insulin deficiency. Due to there not being enough Insulin in the body, the body can't use glucose for energy and instead starts using the fat in the body as energy. This raises glucose levels and produces acidic ketones which are toxic for the body.

Signs of DKA

- Feeling thirsty
- Feeling or being sick
- Blurred vision
- Breathing deeply
- Weeing more
- Feeling tired or confused
- Stomach pains
- Breath smelling of acetone, nail varnish, or pear drops
- High glucose levels

Diagnosis and Treatment

If you develop any of these symptoms, please seek urgent medical care. Ketones are picked up in the urine and your healthcare professional will be able to tell DKA from a urine sample and will provide you with the correct care which may be in a hospital setting if levels are found to be very high.

Acute Illness

If you suffer from an acute illness such as a fever or the flu, it could lead to complications such as dehydration and high glucose levels. Please ask your healthcare team about **sick day rules** - this will tell you what you need to do if you become acutely unwell and will help to reduce complications. There may need to be some changes to your medication whilst your are acutely ill too which the healthcare team should advise you about.

ANNUAL DIABETIC REVIEW

Due to the complications that can arise from Diabetes, all Diabetics should have at least a yearly review with their GP. This should include a blood test and usually a health check with the nurse. During the review, there are **nine key care processes** [12] the GP will look at to assess your risk of Diabetic complications. These are:

·Hba1c - Glucose blood test
·Cholesterol blood test
·Kidney blood test
·Urine sample – to check kidney function for any protein leakage
·Blood pressure
·Diabetic eye test (usually done by an Optometrist)
·Foot check
·Smoking status
·Weight & BMI check

If you are Diabetic, please ensure you have had these checks done in the past year, as they are there to assess and prevent your risk of Diabetic complications. You can also ask for a copy of your blood tests to know what factors you need to improve, and always ask your healthcare professional if there is something you need clarification on. The target ranges of these nine care processes are listed below, if any of the readings are not within range, then this is something that you need to improve, and you can speak to your GP or nurse about how you can achieve the target readings. You can use this page to list your readings to compare how well-controlled your Diabetes is and help identify where you need further support.

Smoking

Smoking can lead to several ill effects, including a higher risk of developing many cancers, especially lung cancer, COPD, heart attacks, and stroke. In addition, if you have Diabetes, you are already at a greater risk of developing heart attacks and stroke. If you are smoking around others, you are also increasing their risk of developing these conditions. Therefore, quitting smoking is essential. You can talk to your healthcare team for further support to help you achieve this.

9 CARE PROCESSES

Care Process	Your Levels	Your Levels	Your Levels
Hba1c (48-58mmol/mol)			
Cholesterol Less than 5mmol/L			
Kidney Function More than eGFR 60mL/min/1.73 m2			
Urine Microalbumin Less than 3 mg/mmol			
Blood Pressure Less than 140/90 mmHg or 130/80mmHg if kidney disease			
Diabetic Eye Test (Should be normal)			
Foot Check (Normal foot pulse & sensation, no issues with feet)			
Smoking Status (Should be a non-smoker)			
Weight & BMI 18.5 to 23 kg/m2 range			

HOME GLUCOSE TESTING

Routine glucose monitoring using a home glucose machine is usually recommended if you are on medication that may cause hypoglycaemia, such as Insulin or Sulfonylureas. For those with a glucose monitoring machine at home, an ideal glucose reading should be between 4-7mmol/l before breakfast. Two hours after a meal, an ideal reading should be 4-9mmol/l.

Have you ever checked the effect different foods have on your glucose levels? To see the impact of food, check your glucose levels two hours after a meal, and note the food you ate and what your sugar levels were. This way, you will notice which foods are raising your glucose levels and which are keeping them regular. Gradually, over time, you can adjust your diet accordingly. Next time try having two chapatis with your usual dal sabzi and check your glucose levels after two hours. Then, the next day, have the same amount of daal sabzi, and this time have one chapati and see the difference this makes to your glucose levels. When checking your glucose levels, please make sure you use a new lancet (needle) each time you test, as this will prevent any infection risk and injury, as using a blunt lancet can be painful. Also, safely dispose of the lancets and used test strips in a yellow sharps bin.

LOOKING AFTER FEET

As a Diabetic, it is crucial to look after your feet. People with diabetes are more prone to circulatory and nerve problems, causing pins and needles, cramps, and numbness in the feet. Diabetics, due to these reasons, have a higher chance of infections which can take longer to heel. If you ever develop foot problems such as cuts or ulcers, show this to a healthcare professional and never self-treat. Check you are wearing the correct footwear, have regular foot checks with your Nurse, Chiropodist or Podiatrist, and be careful to cut your toenails cautiously, don't cut too far down, prevent any cuts, or use a nail file instead. Suppose you are having difficulty cutting your nails. In that case, it is better to have them cut professionally by a Chiropodist or Podiatrist and avoid having them cut at a nail salon due to the increased risk of getting foot infections. Check your feet regularly, and if you notice any problems, even something as small as a little cut, then seek medical help as soon as possible. As mentioned previously, the smallest of scratches on the feet can lead to a severe infection that could result in an amputation.

HEALTHY BLOOD PRESSURE

Blood pressure measures at what force the heart pumps blood around the body. There are two readings:

Systolic pressure – shows at what force the **heart contracts**
Diastolic pressure – shows what force the **heart relaxes**

For a Diabetic, an ideal target blood pressure reading should be less than **135/85mmHg (home setting)** or **140/90mmHg (clinic setting)** [9], and it's essential to have healthy blood pressure due to Diabetics having a greater risk of strokes, heart attacks, and kidney problems. High blood pressure is also known as a silent killer as there are often no symptoms of high blood pressure, so getting your blood pressure checked regularly is essential, and if you are on medication for high blood pressure, never stop taking them unless advised by your Doctor. Here are some of the factors that affect blood pressure:

- **Salt** - for those with high blood pressure, it is crucial to control the amount of salt you have. Salt is essential for our body, but having too much can cause health issues. Don't stop salt from your diet, but control the amount you are having. It's okay to add to dal sabzi when cooking, but don't add extra to your food when you eat these dishes. Salt is a taste that we get used to. The more we consume, the more we get used to that taste and use extra. Many take-out foods and processed foods are high in salt. Even snacks like crisps can have a high salt content, so be mindful and limit these foods. Some chutneys, sauces, and achar are also high in salt, so try to avoid having these regular unless you have prepared them yourselves and have put in a controlled amount of salt. Simple things like not adding salt to chips are a great way to control your salt intake. As per NHS advice, adults should not have more than 6g of salt a day (around 1 level teaspoon). Opting for Himalayan pink salt or rock salt is better than white salt as it is unrefined and contains many more minerals. White salt, on the other hand, often contains additives such as anti-caking agents to prevent the salt from clumping together. A healthy diet with reduced processed and fried food intake will also help reach healthy blood pressure.

- **Exercise** – is a great way to help control your blood pressure, especially if you are overweight.

- **Stress** – the more stressed we are, the more our blood pressure increases. South Asians often suffer stress from family to community influences. We must cut this stress as much as possible, as it harms our health. Exercises such as Yoga breathing exercises are beneficial for reducing stress-induced high blood pressure.

- **Alcohol and Caffeine** - Drinking too much alcohol, tea and coffee can also raise your blood pressure. Even Coke contains caffeine, so control your intake of these drinks.

- **Smoking** - If you are a smoker, it's time to consider quitting smoking, as it can also negatively impact your blood pressure.

- **Water** - Not drinking enough water can increase our blood pressure, try to aim for 6-8 glasses of water (except for those on a fluid-restriction diet).

- **Overweight** - being overweight increases the chance of high blood pressure. Think about the strain on our hearts to pump blood around a larger body. If you are overweight, losing weight will have a positive effect on your blood pressure

Some people suffer from 'white coat syndrome' when it comes to raised blood pressure. This means having a higher blood pressure when you see your Doctor or Nurse as your blood pressure rises just by being in this environment. In this situation, it is better to purchase a blood pressure monitor at home and check your blood pressure at different times of day to get a more accurate reading. You can then present the readings to your Doctor or Nurse to review.

CHOLESTEROL

Cholesterol, a measure of fat in our blood, plays essential roles in maintaining normal body functions. It forms the outer layer of our cells, aids in bile production for fat digestion, provides energy, supports brain function, and facilitates the absorption of fat-soluble vitamins (such as Vitamins A, D, E, and K). However, excessive cholesterol can lead to clogged blood vessels, increasing the risk of heart disease, stroke, and heart attacks—especially for individuals with Diabetes, who face elevated risks. Therefore, maintaining good cholesterol levels as a Diabetic is very important. In addition, South Asians also have a three times higher risk of developing cardiovascular disease [1].

Two primary types of cholesterol exist: LDL (low-density lipoprotein), often referred to as "bad" cholesterol, and HDL (high-density lipoprotein), known as "good" cholesterol. Elevated LDL levels can lead to artery blockages, while HDL helps transport LDL to the liver for breakdown, preventing vessel clogging

Cholesterol levels can be high due to a diet high in saturated fats, excessive consumption of carbohydrates, lack of exercise, stress, and genetic conditions. If you have Diabetes or high cholesterol levels, then, where possible, reduce your dietary fat intake. Swap to having foods with less fat, such as semi-skimmed milk, but where there are no low-fat alternatives, then half the amount of fats you use instead. For example, if there's paneer for dinner, have half of your usual amount of paneer and have more vegetables. If everyone at home uses whole-fat milk, you can still use this milk but dilute it with water instead if your cholesterol levels are high. If having full-fat yogurt, eat half the amount of yogurt that you would usually have. In effect, by reducing your portion size of fatty foods, you also reduce your fat intake.

Many of us like to have achar (pickles) with our desi meals, but these are often preserved in oils – be mindful of this if you have high cholesterol. For those who like butter on their toast, try swapping for spreads with half butter and half rapeseed oil. Choose healthy fats where possible, such as having nuts instead of fried crisps. Cook in oil rather than ghee all the time, and cut out fried foods, crisps, cakes, mithai, and biscuits. These foods are often high in fats. Reduce take-out foods. Fast food burgers, fish and chips, Chinese takeaways, and samosas from local desi shops often contain excessive fat or oil. Enjoy these as occasional treats rather than weekly habits. Many of these dishes can be prepared at home using healthier ingredients and cooking methods.

04

LIFESTYLE

GENETICS

If someone in our family has Type 2 Diabetes, we are also at a higher risk of developing Diabetes. This may be due to a genetic factor or our lifestyles. From a genetic perspective, South Asians are more likely to have reduced beta cell function of the pancreatic cells, leading to less Insulin production [13]. We are also more likely to store more visceral fat (fat around the waist) [14]. This visceral fat is thought to coat our organs with fat in the abdominal area and reduce the effectiveness of the organs. One critical organ located in this area is the Pancreas which produces Insulin.

From a lifestyle perspective, the diet we have seen our parents consume is the diet we are more likely to follow. Our food tastes become similar, for this is what we have known and where our comfort lies. Similarly, we sometimes follow their path of physical activity too, and if they have a sedentary lifestyle, we may have picked up on this too and become less active.

Our genes may raise our risk of developing certain health conditions, but our lifestyle choices can help prevent this. We cannot change our genetics, but there are many things we can do to improve our lifestyles, and sometimes the simplest of changes can have the most impact. We don't need to stop our traditional foods. Instead, we need to adapt them to ways that are healthier for us. There's no age for change, and the quicker we make changes, the better it will be for our overall health. If we don't make time for our health now, then in years to come, our health may suffer because of the choices we made and we are forced to make time for an illness that could have been prevented.

As South Asians, our genetics may predispose us to Diabetes, but whether that genetic switch is activated depends on our lifestyle choices. By making positive changes, we can effectively turn off that switch.

MAKING TIME FOR HEALTH

During my Diabetes educational classes, I often hear attendees express the struggle of finding time for themselves. Juggling many responsibilities, caring for children, grandchildren, cooking, and cleaning which leaves little room for self-care. But I remind them that neglecting their health now could lead to future challenges. Who would care for them if their health deteriorated? The chores would pile up, and their well-being would suffer. Investing time in our health is crucial; procrastination isn't an option.

One thing to consider is our screen time, we spend hours in front of TVs or scrolling through our phones. Yet, can't we spare at least 20 minutes for our health? Most phones even track screen time—take a look at yours. What does it reveal about your priorities?

Sometimes, all we need is a gentle nudge in the right direction. The younger generation find it easier to attend a gym or join exercise classes and will make time for these activities. But our parents and grandparents may feel lost. Offering support whether it's taking over cooking duties for a day or going for family walks can kickstart their healthy journey. Small gestures matter.

Don't regret not prioritizing your health. The future lies in your hands. Start today; simple changes can yield significant results. Tomorrow isn't guaranteed for everyone. Make today the day you create positive habits.

HEALTHY WEIGHT

There was a time our lives were more active, demanding greater energy to match our physical exertion. However, in today's lifestyle, we've increased our food intake while significantly reducing our physical activity. The consequences are far-reaching. In the past, we walked to most places whether to local shops or to drop off our kids at school. Now, we rely on cars even for short distances. Our sedentary habits and dependence on technology have led to weight gain, contributing to the rise in conditions like Diabetes and obesity.

Here is a simple formula to help understand healthy weight:

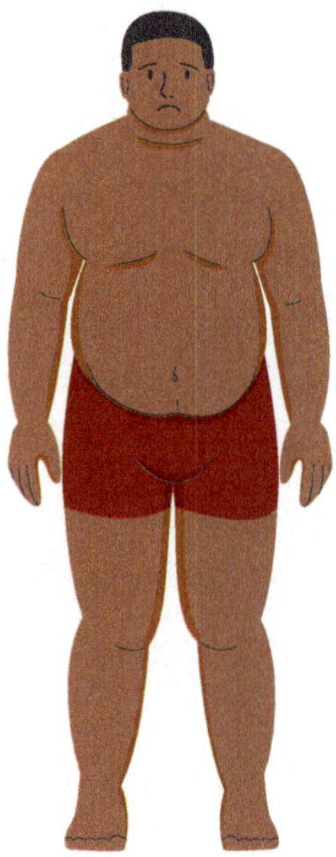

Energy consumed from **food** is **more than** energy used for **physical activity** = **weight gain**

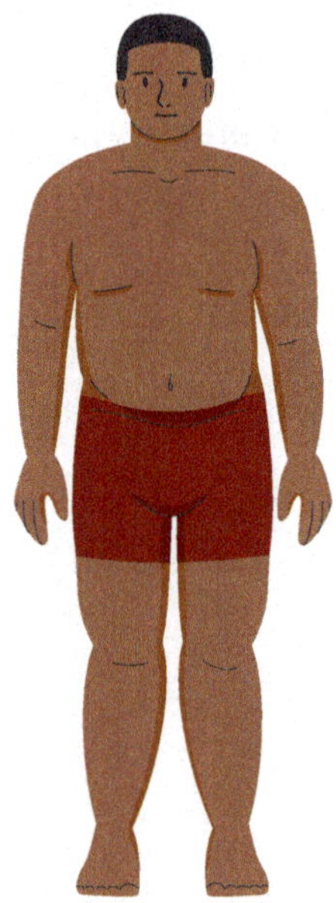

Energy consumed from **food** is the **same** as energy used for **physical activity** = **stable weight**

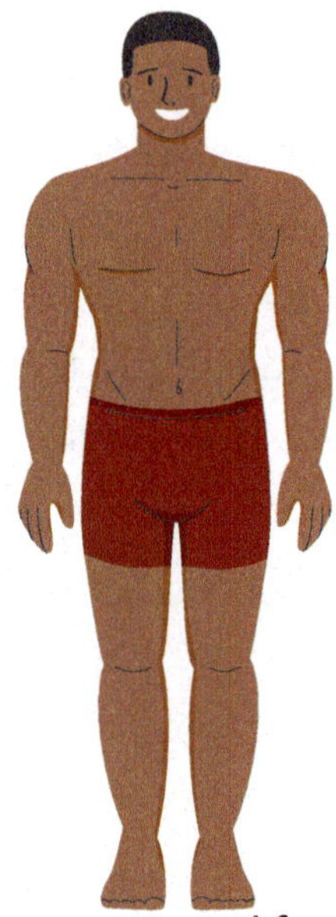

Energy consumed from **food** is **less than** energy used for **physical activity** = **weight loss**

Therefore, in order to lose weight we need to burn more energy than we eat. To keep weight stable, our energy from food needs to match our energy usage, and to gain weight, we need to eat more food and use less energy. Calories inform us how much energy is in a particular food. So how many calories do we need per day?

Men - 2500kcal
Women 2000kcal

This is an average intake. However, the amount depends on age, physical activity, weight, and height. Let's look at an example of calories and exercise. A gulab jamun contains around 232 calories, to burn off 232 calories, we would need to do the following amount of activity [30]:

1.4 hours of cleaning

35 minutes cycling

23 minutes of running

Today many of us are eating more calories than what we are burning through physical activity, which is causing weight gain, and as a result, there are a higher number of people that are overweight or obese.

If we look at our lifestyle today, most of our time is spent sitting down, sitting at our desks, sitting on the sofa watching TV, sitting and using our phones, and driving to get where we need to go. We need to keep our bodies moving and aim to **exercise at least 30 minutes a day, five days a week**. This could be going out for walks, walking up and down your living room, jogging, gym, dancing, workouts, exercise videos - whatever you can do, please do. Not only will this cut your risk/complications of Diabetes, certain cancers, and heart disease, but it will also improve your mental health as exercise releases endorphins, the happy hormone.

Many of us lead busy lives, juggling work, family responsibilities, and household chores. Finding time for exercise can be challenging, but even small steps can significantly improve our health.

Consider these strategies:

1. **Treadmill in the Living Room**: During winter months, place a treadmill in your living room. You can exercise while enjoying your favorite TV show.
2. **Lunch Break Walks**: If you're at work, use part of your lunch break for a walk. Even 10 minutes of brisk walking can make a difference.
3. **Family Walks**: After evening meals, consider going for family walks. It's a great way to bond and stay active.
4. **Timing Matters**: Our heaviest meal is often dinner, followed by TV time. To prevent weight gain, aim for early dinners (around 6 pm). This leaves the evening for some physical activity.
5. **Home Habits**: If you work from home, use the downstairs toilet if your workspace is upstairs. Opt for smaller glasses when drinking water—this encourages more trips to the kitchen.
6. **Walk and Talk**: Make a habit of walking while on phone calls. These small adjustments gradually increase our activity levels and contribute to weight management.

In addition to keeping active, eating the correct foods is essential to maintain a healthy weight. All foods contain calories, but did you know that fat contains more calories than protein and carbohydrates? **1g of fat will provide nine calories,** whereas **1 gram of protein provides four calories,** and **1g of carbohydrate also contains four calories**. Fat has more than double the amount of calories (energy) compared to protein and carbohydrates. The more fatty, fried foods we consume, the more likely we are to put on weight, so try to limit the intake of these foods as not only will they increase our weight, but they can also cause high cholesterol if consumed regularly. Simple changes like grilling food instead of frying or not putting butter on chapatis will reduce our fat intake. Eventually, these small changes will start to make a difference.

If you are overweight, reducing weight will help with controlling your Diabetes as well as lowering your glucose levels.

OBESITY

Obesity is believed to account for 80-85% of Type 2 Diabetes cases [15]. While some individuals may become overweight or obese due to health conditions (such as an underactive thyroid or physical injuries), many others develop obesity from poor lifestyle choices—such as neglecting their health, consuming unhealthy foods, and leading sedentary lives. In the UK, approximately 1 in 4 people are obese, and 31.2% of children aged 2-15 are already affected by obesity [15]. Obesity is associated with various health conditions, including heart disease, certain cancers, osteoarthritis, liver disease, and sleep apnea. By adopting healthier eating habits and increasing physical activity, we can not only combat obesity but also mitigate its associated health risks.

MAKING CHANGES FOR LIFE

Often, we strive to lose weight for specific events—like weddings or vacations. We diligently eat healthily and exercise until we reach our goal, only to slip back into old habits once the event has passed. Unfortunately, our hard work often goes to waste, and we find ourselves back at our original weight. Instead of treating healthy living as a temporary fix, we should integrate it into our daily lives. Long-term lifestyle improvements are more effective than quick diet fixes.

Many people resort to meal replacements - shakes and soups, instead of regular healthy meals. These processed foods, which transform from powder to liquid with water, raise questions about their preservatives, additives, and impact on our health. Rather than relying on such shortcuts, we should focus on gradual changes to our eating habits. Small steps like reducing daily biscuit consumption or swapping unhealthy snacks for nuts add up over time. Eventually, these adjustments become our new normal, leading to a healthier version of ourselves. Consistently maintaining these changes ensures our well-being in the years ahead.

EXERCISE

Exercise offers numerous health benefits, including stress reduction, bone-strengthening (which helps prevent fractures), and the prevention of age-related muscle loss, cancer, heart disease, and obesity. It also ranks among the best strategies for preventing diabetes and managing its complications. Regular exercise prompts our body to utilise excess glucose and fat as energy.

The best part? Exercise doesn't require spending money - it's free! Despite being aware of these health advantages, many of us miss out on physical activity. Exercise takes various forms, from dancing and gardening to swimming, walking, football, yoga, and badminton. Any activity that leaves you breathless qualifies as moderate-intensity exercise. Aim for at least 30 minutes of this type of exercise on five days a week or 20 minutes daily.

How much exercise?

30 minutes 5 days a week
or
20 minutes 7 days a week

If you're able to engage in more exercise, that's even better! Just like with muscles, the saying holds true for our heart: 'If you don't use it, you lose it.' Did you realize that our heart is also a muscle? Exercise plays a crucial role in strengthening our heart muscles and enhancing lung function.

When we engage in regular moderate-intensity exercise, our heart starts pumping more efficiently, leading to improved blood circulation throughout our bodies. Additionally, exercise generates heat, making it an excellent way to stay a little warmer during chilly winter months. Moreover, consistent moderate-intensity exercise helps lower glucose levels, reduces high blood pressure, and contributes to healthier cholesterol levels.

How does exercise affect glucose levels?

- Increased sensitivity to Insulin - meaning the effect of Insulin increases so more glucose can be converted into energy for the muscles to use
- The contraction of the muscles allows the cells to take up more glucose
- Once we finish moderate or high-intensity exercise, our body continues to burn off the excess glucose even hours after stopping exercise
- Combination of these factors reduces the glucose levels in the blood
- To see the benefit of exercise, check your glucose levels before activity and then after exercise (make sure levels are not dropping below 4mmol/l)

If you are on Insulin or a Sulfonylurea medication, too much exercise may lead to hypos, especially if you have not eaten enough carbohydrates, so please be mindful of this and ensure you check your glucose levels before exercise. If they are less than 5.5mmol/l, have a carbohydrate snack before exercising. It may also be wise to recheck your glucose levels after the exercise to ensure levels are normal and always carry something sweet with you in case of hypos.

Establishing a daily exercise routine is crucial for maintaining our healthiest lives. Consider motivating the entire family to engage in physical activity. Older individuals may lack confidence in venturing out for exercise, so providing support is essential. Going for walks together or participating in exercise classes as a family can be beneficial. As we grow up, our parents also age, and they may require that extra support. A Study carried out by Sporting England found that many of us are not hitting the recommended exercise targets. Their key findings were [31]:

- **South Asian women were less active than South Asian men**
- **74% of South Asian women undertake less than 30 minutes of physical activity a week**
- **South Asians are less physically active than the White British population**

Even more, reason to motivate the elders in our families. For those of you with children, consider incorporating exercise into your family routine. When kids engage in physical activity from a young age, they're more likely to continue these habits later in life. As parents, we serve as the primary role models for our children, and they often emulate our behaviours. Personally, I've followed in my parents' active footsteps.
Join in on the sports or activities that your kids enjoy. It's not only an opportunity for us to learn something new but also a chance to bond with them. Whether it's dancing to music, doing some bhangra, or simply running around in the garden together, spending quality time with family, whether parents, siblings, partners, or children are precious. Especially in our busy lives, these moments create lasting connections.

During summertime, we become more active as the weather is better and days are longer, so make the most of this season, go for evening walks or do some activities in the garden. Gardening is another great way to relieve stress, and growing your fruits and vegetables is another way to stay active during the summer months, with the added benefit of having your home-grown organic produce to make delicious foods. For many of us, farming is something our grandparents and ancestors did so easily, but now we have lost touch with nature, and even our gardens have become concrete jungles.

During winter, when we spend more time indoors, it's essential to maintain our exercise routines. Fortunately, there are plenty of free exercises we can do at home. Consider putting on your favourite song and dancing—it's a fun way to stay active. Alternatively, explore home workout videos on YouTube (check the resources section for links) that you can follow from the comfort of your living room. You can even challenge yourself by walking up and down the stairs or covering the entire length of your house—count the steps to see how far you've gone.

Balancing exercise with full-time jobs and family commitments can be tough. Try waking up a bit earlier to fit in a workout or practice some yoga. Utilise your lunch break at work for a quick exercise session. For parents, exercising with your kids after work not only benefits your health but also strengthens family bonds.

If long exercise sessions feel daunting, break it down into manageable chunks. Aim for three 10-minute sessions throughout the day—after breakfast, lunch, and dinner—adding up to the recommended 30 minutes daily. Try exercise snacks - running on the spot while the kettle boils or doing leg raises while washing up. Consistency is key; as you exercise regularly, increasing intensity becomes easier. Even if mobility is a concern, simple activities like sitting and standing a few times activate leg muscles. Reflect on your exercise preferences and whether you're meeting your daily targets. How can you carve out time from your busy schedule? Transform exercise into a daily habit, and your future health will thank you.

Additionally, as we age, incorporating strengthening exercises becomes crucial. These exercises bolster bones and prevent fractures. Falls are common among the elderly, leading to sedentary lifestyles during recovery. To avoid this, try strength training at least twice a week. It can be as straightforward as using small weights or holding cans of beans in each hand or even carrying heavy shopping bags around town.

Here are some examples of what counts as moderate intensity exercise and some strengthening and balance exercise from the Government website [16].

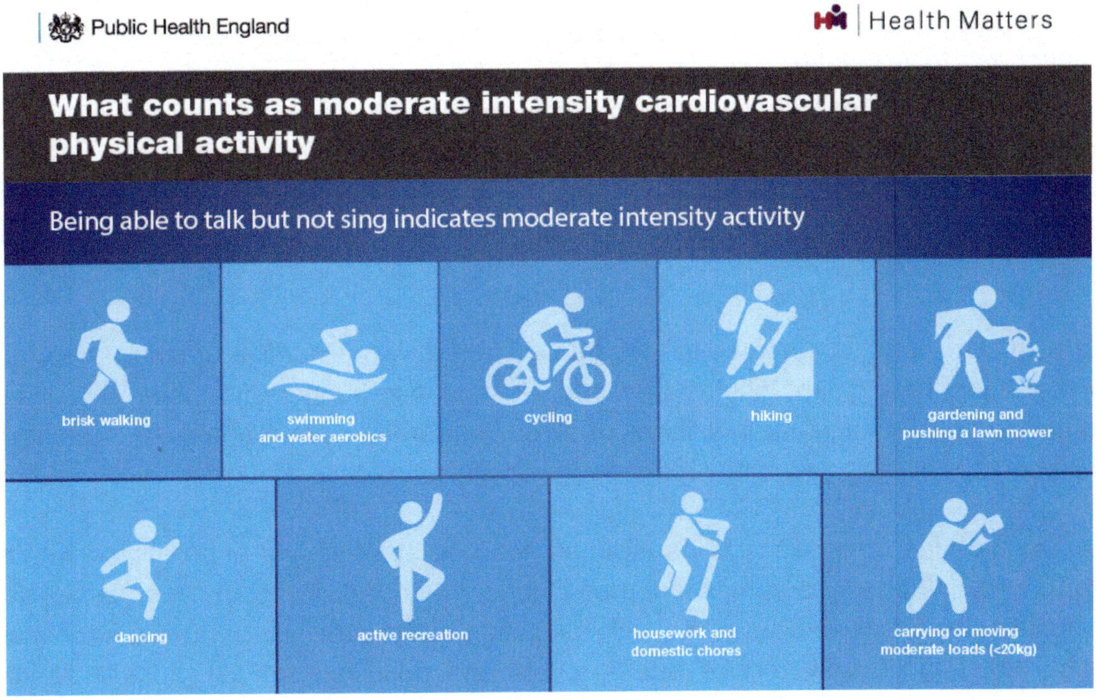

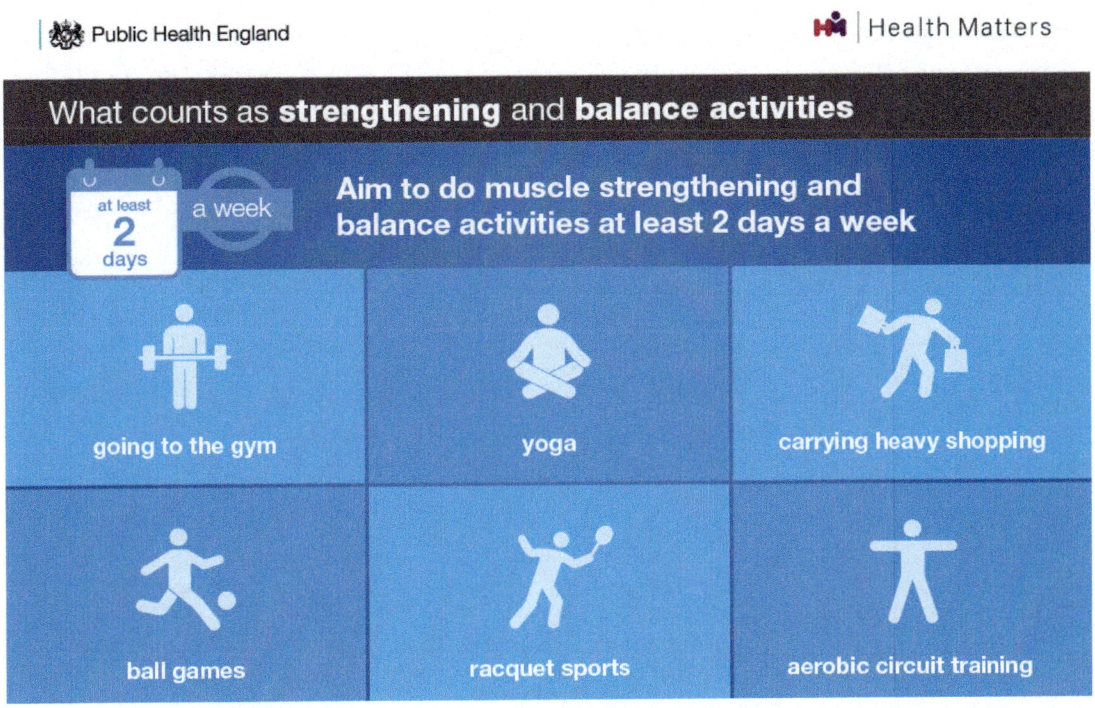

STRESS AND GLUCOSE LEVELS

Cortisol, a hormone produced in response to stress, has several effects on our bodies. One of these effects is an increase in glucose production, meaning that the more stressed we are, the higher our glucose levels become. As South Asians, we often overthink about others and absorb their stress, which negatively impacts our health. While some factors in life are beyond our control, it's essential to set boundaries to protect our happiness. If something makes you unhappy, don't hesitate to voice your opinion. Bottling up emotions can lead to poor mental health, so seek support from others to alleviate tension and gain clarity.

Lack of sleep also contributes to elevated cortisol levels. Prioritise getting a good night's rest and plenty of sleep. Insufficient sleep can increase hunger and make us more prone to snacking. Aim for at least 8 hours of sleep, with particular emphasis on the two hours between 10 PM and midnight—the most beneficial time for rest.

On the flip side, exercise acts as a stress antidote by releasing endorphins—the 'happy hormones.' These endorphins suppress cortisol production, promoting calmness and optimism. Regular exercise, along with relaxation techniques like breathing exercises and yoga, can significantly reduce stress levels and positively impact glucose regulation. Consider incorporating yoga poses like Mandukasana which is said to stimulate the pancreas and improve Insulin release [17], but always learn from a qualified yoga teacher.

Massage, an ancient South Asian practice, is another effective way to de-stress and relax. Unfortunately, we often neglect it. Regular massages improve joint mobility and overall relaxation. You can easily incorporate massage into your daily routine by using oil to massage your skin before bathing (be cautious to avoid slippery surfaces). For diabetic patients dealing with reduced circulation, regular massage offers immunity-boosting benefits and improves blood flow.

GIFTS

South Asians have a longstanding tradition of exchanging gifts during celebrations. Whether it's Diwali, Vaisakhi, Eid, a birthday, or a wedding, we rarely attend these events empty-handed. Instead, we offer sweet treats ranging from mithai (Indian sweets) to chocolate boxes and tins of biscuits during Christmas. Many of us can relate to accumulating surplus boxes of these goodies, often passing them along to others.
However, gifting sweets to individuals with diabetes poses a challenge. When presented with a box of mithai that must be consumed promptly before it spoils, the recipient faces a dilemma: indulge and risk elevated glucose levels or decline and risk appearing ungrateful. Politeness often prevails, leading us to accept the gift, even if it means managing our blood sugar afterwards. In such situations, consider sharing the mithai with family and friends.

Another issue arises when we feel compelled to give a full kilogram of mithai, regardless of household size. The pressure of 'what will people say' drives this behaviour. But perhaps it's time to break free from this expectation. Next time you visit a Desi sweet shop to buy a gift, pause and reflect. Does the recipient have diabetes? How many people live in their home? Could a healthier alternative like fruits, nuts, flowers, plants, or candles be more thoughtful?

When our daughter was born, my husband and I decided to celebrate differently. Instead of mithai, we gifted houseplants specifically air-purifying plants to help improve health of others. In addition we donated money to a girls orphanage in India - Unique Home so that we could help improve the lives of other beautiful children in this world. While change may spark conversations, someone with an open mind will appreciate the gesture. Perhaps, over time, we'll establish a healthier trend. After all, change has to begin somewhere.

DIABETES & FUTURE GENERATIONS

Type 2 Diabetes is increasingly affecting younger individuals, particularly among South Asians. While it used to be associated with those over 40, the risk of developing Type 2 Diabetes now emerges as early as age 25 [28]. Shockingly I have even witnessed children as young as ten receiving a diagnosis of this condition.

Following a Diabetes diagnosis, complications often arise, typically about a decade after the initial diagnosis. These complications correlate with deteriorating glucose levels and can manifest earlier or later based on health and glucose control. If children are diagnosed with Type 2 Diabetes at age 10, we may witness complications by their 20s - eye issues, heightened heart attack risk in their 30s, and kidney disease in their 40s. Is this the future we want for our children? In addition to this, the life expectancy of a Type 2 diabetic could be reduced by up to 10 years [32]. By making changes now we can help to increase that life expectancy for more healthier years ahead. Making lifestyle changes is essential not only for ourselves but also our families, ensuring their well-being too.

Reflect on our childhood compared to today's children. We grew up without mobile phones or iPads, spending hours playing actively in the garden. Unfortunately, today's kids lack that level of physical activity. As parents, we must encourage their involvement. Children often emulate our behaviour, if they see us glued to screens, they'll follow suit. Conversely, if they witness us exercising, they'll likely join in. Visit the park, play in the backyard, grab badminton rackets or a football, these activities boost physical activity and release endorphins, those delightful 'feel-good' hormones. The more consistently we engage in these habits, the more ingrained they become for everyone.

Moreover, we urgently need Diabetes education for young children, especially in schools. Equipping them with knowledge about food and drink choices from a young age empowers them to make healthier decisions throughout life.

05

DIET

DIET

The consumption of wholesome, unprocessed foods has significantly declined, a stark contrast to the traditional South Asian diets of our ancestors. In their era, food was often cultivated at home, free from pesticides, and meals were crafted from scratch with fresh ingredients each day. In contrast, modern households often rely on freezers stocked with processed and pre-packaged foods.

As our lives have grown increasingly hectic, our eating habits have shifted towards convenience. Yet, if we were to cut down on screen time, we could redirect that time towards preparing nutritious meals or engaging in physical activity. Embracing aspects of our grandparents' simpler lifestyle could potentially lead to a substantial decrease in Type 2 Diabetes cases prevalent today. It's a common narrative that our ancestors cooked with ghee and led healthy lives. Indeed, ghee can be part of a healthy diet if coupled with an active lifestyle. However, indulging in calorie-dense foods without sufficient physical activity can lead to health issues. Moderation and regular exercise can help us harness the energy from these foods and minimize fat storage. A diverse diet, rich in fresh foods, is the cornerstone of good health, providing a variety of nutrients that are beneficial to our well-being. On busy days, when processed foods are the go-to, it's important to balance them with vegetables or a side salad. The proliferation of food outlets has made take-out more accessible than ever, a significant shift from my younger days when such options were scarce. This convenience has led to a decline in home cooking and an increase in dining out, even among schoolchildren who are growing accustomed to fast food. In our grandparents' time, treats like mithai and samosa were reserved for special occasions, unlike the constant availability we see now, which is another factor in the healthier lifestyles they led.

This chapter delves into the importance of diet in managing Diabetes and maintaining stable blood glucose levels. It aims to enhance your understanding of the various food groups and guide you towards making more informed and healthier dietary choices.

SUGAR

Sugar is available in various forms, such as sucrose, commonly found in household sugar and added to numerous foods and beverages, fructose, which is the natural sugar in fruits, and lactose, the sugar present in milk. Sugars can also be white or brown in colour. A widespread belief is that brown sugar, jaggery (gur shakkar), or honey is healthier than white sugar due to supposedly lower sugar content. However, all these sweeteners contain comparable amounts of sucrose. Therefore, the notion that individuals with Diabetes can consume unlimited amounts of gur shakkar is incorrect. The primary advantage of choosing gur shakkar over white sugar is its unrefined nature, which means it retains more vitamins and nutrients. Nevertheless, those with Diabetes should still moderate their sugar intake, whether it's in beverages or sweet treats like mithais, chocolates, or biscuits.

The allure of sugar is strong; the more we consume, the more we crave its sweetness. Consider tea, for instance: the more sugar we add, the more accustomed we become to its sweet flavor, making it challenging to enjoy unsweetened tea. Many people feel the need to indulge in sugary items daily or even multiple times a day, but this is often due to habit rather than necessity. It's important to note that our bodies do not require added sugar, as glucose is naturally produced from the carbohydrates we consume. Introducing extra sugary foods and drinks only increases our overall glucose intake.

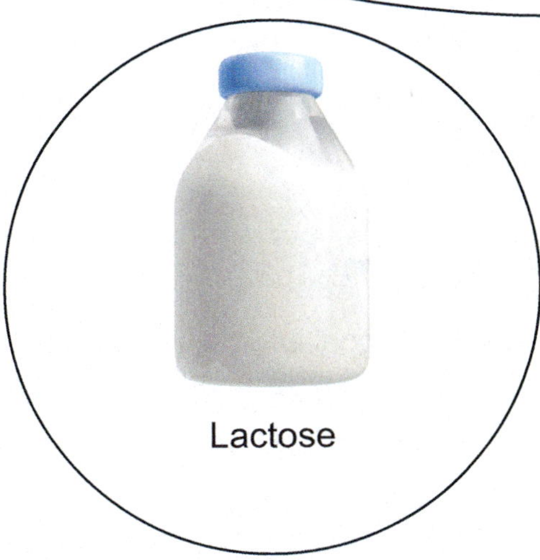

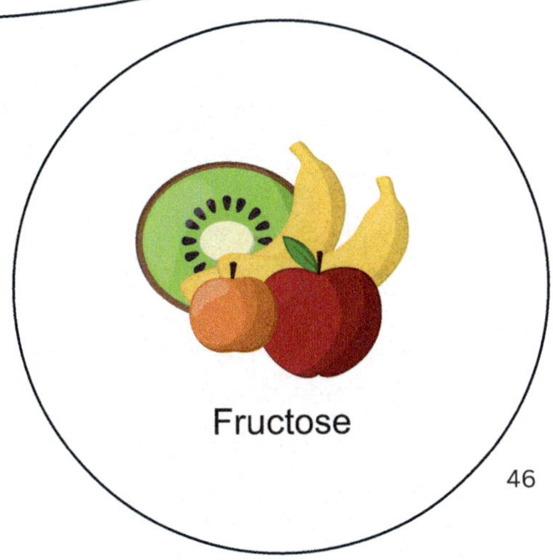

SUGARY TREATS

The maximum recommended daily allowance of sugar is seven spoons a day, and if you have Diabetes, aim for even less than this. Seven spoons of sugar seem like a lot, but many foods contain sugar without us realising it. A can of baked beans can contain up to four spoons of sugar, one tablespoon of Tamarind (Imli) sauce contains two spoons of sugar, a rusk has two and a half spoons of sugar, and a can of coke has nearly nine spoons of sugar. Before we know it, these sugars add up, and without realising, we have consumed more than the recommended daily allowance. Many of us crave a sugary treat, and being Diabetic doesn't have to mean you have to stop all your treats. Instead, set a limit and have these as an occasional treat once or twice a week as a small portion. It's when we make these sugary foods daily habits that they start to cause issues like having a can of Coke every day or having biscuits or mithai with chai every day. It is all about portion control, such as having a small piece of chocolate instead of finishing the whole chocolate bar. Another way to reduce our sugary foods is to stop buying them. We won't be tempted to eat it if it's not in the house.

If you are craving something sweet, it is better to have a piece of fruit or a date or a small portion of raisins than consume foods such as biscuits that have had sugar added to them as the naturally sweet foods have a lower glycaemic index and will increase blood glucose levels slower than foods with added sugar.

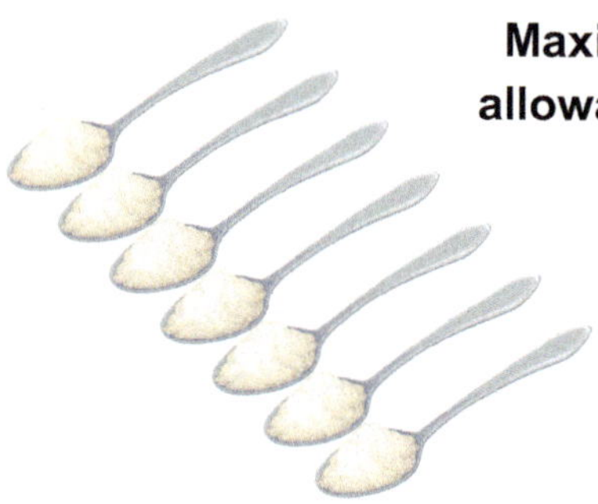

Maximum recommeded daily allowance of sugar is 7 spoons

1 teaspoon of sugar is 4g of sugar

Next time you reach for a chocolate, have a look at the nutritional information, how many grams of sugar does it read? Simply divide this amount by 4 and you will know how many spoons of sugar in the item. For example a chocolate contains 12g of sugar, dividing this by 4 will give us 3, so it contains 3 spoons of sugar.

HOW MANY SPOONS OF SUGAR?

Here are a few common foods/drinks examples to show you how much sugar they contain on average [18]:

Rooh Afza

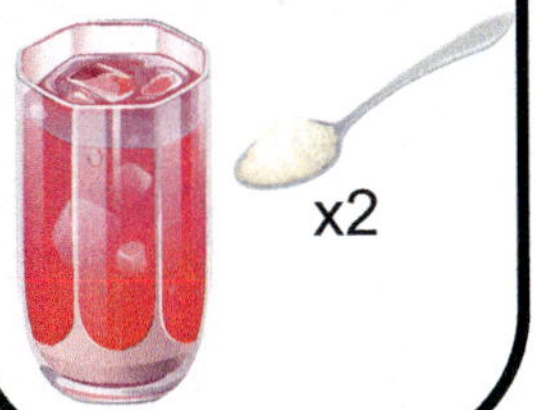

x2

1 Barfi

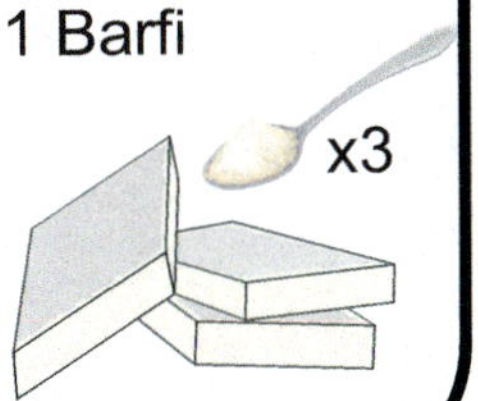

x3

Jalebi

x5

1 Laddoo

x4

Halwa

x4

Coke

x9

1 piece Rusk

x2.5

Chocolate Digestive Biscuit

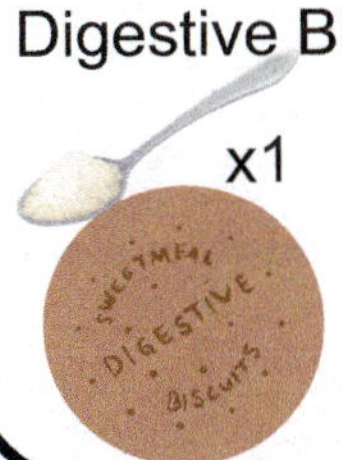

x1

1 piece Bounty Chocolate

x3.5

Medium Mcdonalds Milkshake

x14

CARBOHYDRATES

The three primary macronutrients essential for our body are Fats, Proteins, and Carbohydrates, each serving a unique function. Carbohydrates act as the main fuel for our bodies, converting into glucose upon consumption to provide energy. Consuming carbohydrates beyond our body's energy requirements can lead to elevated blood glucose levels and, if this pattern persists, it may heighten the risk of developing Type 2 Diabetes, particularly in sedentary individuals.

What constitutes Carbohydrates? Starchy foods are the predominant sources of carbohydrates, including staples like roti, rice, potatoes, bread, pasta, pizza, cereals, as well as snacks like samosas, pakoras, spring rolls, and noodles.

Additionally, many sweetened foods are rich in carbohydrates, such as cakes, biscuits, sweets, beverages, and chocolates. Carbohydrates are also naturally found in fruits (e.g., apples, bananas), vegetables (e.g., carrots, pumpkins), and dairy products like milk and yogurt, as well as in pulses like daals. While these foods break down into varying amounts of glucose, they also offer a range of other nutrients; for instance, yogurt provides fat and protein, and daal is a good source of protein. The following page will illustrate the impact of different carbohydrate-rich foods on blood glucose levels.

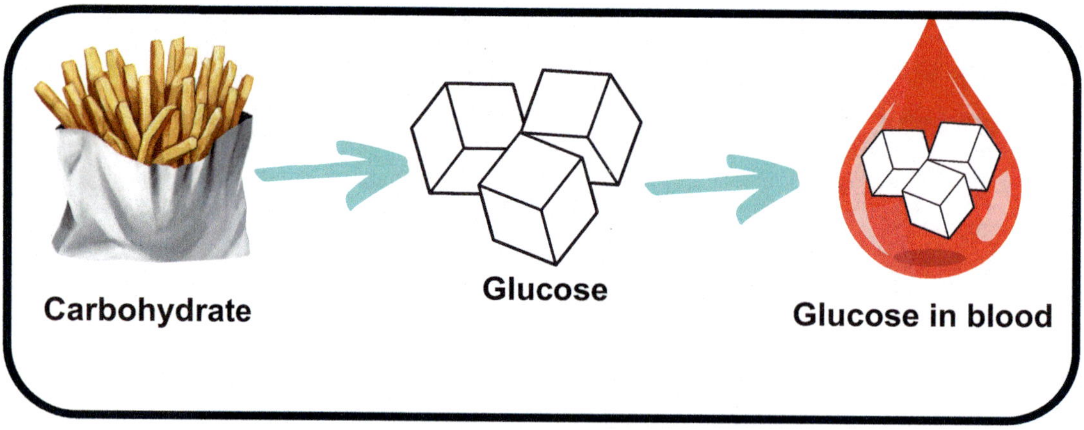

300g tadka daal
= 38g carb
= effect of 8 spoons of sugar

300g daal makhani
= 25g carb
= effect of 5 spoons of sugar

100g basmati rice
= 32g carb
= effect of 6 spoons of sugar

30g small chapati
=13g carb
= effect of 3 spoons of sugar

100g aloo paratha
= 32g carb
= effect of 6 spoons of sugar

85g naan bread
= 43g carb
= effect of 9 spoons of sugar

100g dosa
= 40g carb
= effect of 8 spoons of sugar

200g aloo gobi
= 18g carb
= effect of 4 spoons of sugar

200g aloo sabzi
= 37g carb
= effect of 7 spoons of sugar

120g Samosa
= 33g carb
= effect of 7 spoons of sugar

Here are some examples of the carbohydrate content in Desi foods and the effect they have on blood sugar levels. For more examples see the Carbs & Cals World Foods book or app [19]

70g veg pizza slice
= 25g carb
= effect of 5 spoons of sugar

100g oven chips
= 30g carb
= effect of 6 spoons of sugar

22g of 1 garlic bread piece
= 10g carb
= effect of 2 spoons of sugar

44g thick white bread
=20g carb
= effect of 4 spoons of sugar

170g pasta
= 34g carb
= effect of 7 spoons of sugar

136g cassava chips
= 71g carb
= effect of 14 spoons of sugar

115g noodles
= 41g carb
= effect of 8 spoons of sugar

264g chicken pie
= 55g carb
= effect of 11 spoons of sugar

158g veggie burger
= 42g carb
= effect of 8 spoons of sugar

Here are some examples of the carbohydrate content in some other common foods and the effect they have on blood sugar levels. See the Carbs & Cals Calorie Counter book or app for more examples. [29]

Frequent overindulgence in carbohydrates and sugary treats can heighten the risk of developing Type 2 Diabetes. However, the solution isn't to eliminate carbohydrates altogether, as they are the main source of energy for our bodies. The key is to opt for healthier carbohydrate options and to align our portion sizes with our energy needs. The glycaemic index (GI) is a helpful term that measures how rapidly foods can elevate our blood glucose levels. In general terms:

High GI foods lead to a quicker rise in blood sugar levels.
Low GI foods result in a slower increase in blood sugar levels.

High GI foods typically include simple carbohydrates like white bread, doughnuts, and cake, which are quickly broken down into glucose. On the other hand, low GI foods, such as porridge and wholemeal bread, are complex carbohydrates. These contain more fibre, vitamins, and minerals, and they help us feel fuller for extended periods.

If we visualize carbohydrates as a string of beads, complex carbohydrates would be akin to long, thick strings, while simple carbohydrates would resemble short, thin ones. The beads represent glucose molecules. Simple carbohydrates, being shorter chains, rapidly disintegrate into glucose, spiking our blood sugar levels. Conversely, complex carbohydrates, with their longer chains, take more time to convert into glucose, thus gradually raising blood sugar levels. For those managing Diabetes, it's advisable to favour low GI foods over high GI ones. This approach helps prevent abrupt spikes in glucose levels, supports the gradual release of insulin, and aids in preventing insulin resistance. Additionally, low-GI foods contribute to prolonged satiety, which can help curb the urge to snack.

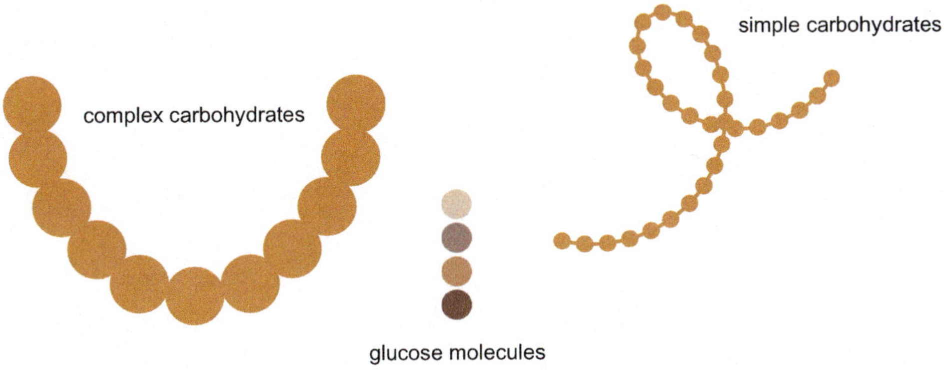

At mealtime, it's advisable to prioritize complex carbohydrates, which are digested slowly and provide a sustained energy release. Examples of complex carbohydrates include wholemeal chapati, brown rice, quinoa, oats, dal, chickpeas, vegetables, wholemeal pasta, and cornmeal. In contrast, simple carbohydrates, such as white bread, pasta, pies, pastries, and samosas, often carry 'empty calories' - they're high in fats and sugars but low in nutritional value. Foods like cakes and biscuits may satisfy a sweet tooth but contribute little beyond increased fat and sugar levels. Complex carbohydrates, however, are rich in fibre, supporting heart health and aiding digestion.

Individuals with active lifestyles those who exercise regularly, work out at the gym, are pregnant, or have physically demanding jobs like construction require more carbohydrates for energy compared to someone who spends the day sedentary, such as watching movies or working at a desk. It's important to adjust carbohydrate portion sizes according to our activity levels. For example, starting a relaxed Sunday with aloo parathas may result in the body storing more energy as fat rather than using it.

Carbohydrates consumed are transformed into glucose for energy. Excess glucose is stored in the liver as glycogen, and when these stores are full, additional sugar is converted into fat, particularly visceral fat around the abdominal organs. This can lead to conditions like fatty liver and impede the pancreas's function, contributing to insulin resistance - a factor in Type 2 Diabetes. High cholesterol can also result from excess glucose being turned into fat.

When deciding on carbohydrate portions, consider your activity plans for the day and choose an amount that matches your expected energy expenditure. A balanced meal should include not only carbohydrates but also moderate amounts of fats and a substantial serving of protein.

When planning your main meals, it's best to include just one type of carbohydrate. Often, we pile on multiple carbohydrate sources in a single meal, leading to a spike in blood sugar levels. For instance, pairing pizza with sides like chips and garlic bread triples your carbohydrate intake. Similarly, a meal of chapati, rice, and potato curry combines three carbohydrate sources. Focusing on one complex carbohydrate per meal can help maintain satiety for a longer period.

Portion control can be guided by healthy eating plates available for purchase. Fareeha Jay has designed an illustrative Desi portion control plate, which is featured later in this book. Ideally, carbohydrates should constitute only about a quarter to a third of your meal plate, with the remainder filled with vegetables, salads, proteins, and a small amount of fat. For Western meals, follow the healthy eating template, and for South Asian meals, use the thaali system for portion management.

Refined Carbohydrates

Refined carbohydrates are those that have been processed and stripped of their natural state. Take white flour, for example, which in its natural form as wholemeal flour (or 'kanak' in Punjabi) contains the outer bran and germ. This processing removes valuable fibre, minerals, vitamins, and some proteins, leaving behind white flour. Some processed flours are 'fortified' with added vitamins post-processing. However, starting with wholemeal or wholesome foods is inherently more beneficial. Refined carbohydrate products include items like pizza, samosas, naan bread, pies, white bread, and pastries. Opting for wholemeal or wholegrain alternatives is advisable, as they are less processed, more nutrient-dense, and promote longer-lasting fullness due to their slower breakdown into glucose compared to white flour products. Nowadays, there are wholemeal versions of many products, including bread, pasta, noodles, and brown rice. Always choose these wholemeal options when shopping for better overall health. Unfortunately, the refining process extends beyond carbohydrates to other foods such as sugar, oil, and salt, often for aesthetic reasons, but this comes at the expense of our health, a fact that remains unnoticed by many.

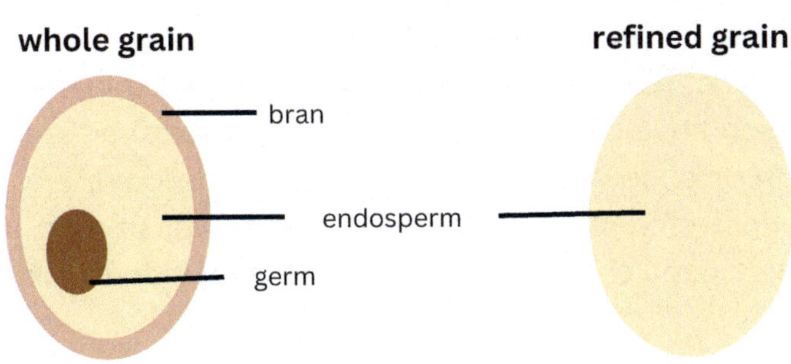

PROTEIN

Protein plays a crucial role in our bodies, contributing to muscle development, energy production, hormone synthesis, and tissue repair. It is one of the main nutriments that our body cannot make. If your body does not have enough protein daily, then it will break down existing muscle.

When we consume protein-rich foods, they are broken down into amino acids. While our bodies can produce some amino acids, there are nine essential amino acids that we must obtain from our diet.

Complete proteins, found in foods such as quinoa, dairy, eggs, fish, and soy, contain all nine essential amino acids. Protein is described as the macro nutrient most likely to make us feel fuller and satisfied after a meal [33]. Including protein in our meals can prevent overeating, leading to better weight management. To enhance glucose control, consider incorporating more protein into your diet. Rather than relying solely on carbohydrates for energy, aim for approximately 0.75 grams of protein per kilogram of body weight. For instance, if you weigh 80 kilograms, your daily protein intake should be around 60 grams. While many individuals who consume eggs, meat, and fish meet their protein needs, some South Asians following vegetarian diets may fall short. During meals, consciously choose protein sources for your plate.

As we age, protein becomes even more critical to prevent muscle loss and maintain mobility. Pair protein consumption with muscle-strengthening exercises to improve overall strength.

Here are some ways to boost protein intake:

1. Nuts, Seeds, and Dairy: Incorporate nuts, seeds, milk, and yogurt into your diet.
2. Lentils and Legumes: South Asian dishes often include lentils (dal), chana, kidney beans which are good protein sources.
3. Vegetarian Options: Add peas, edamame beans, chickpeas, kidney beans, and seeds to pasta, rice, or salads.
4. Smart Snacking: Opt for nuts or nut butter on whole-grain toast instead of sugary spreads.
5. Chapatis with a Twist: Mix besan (chickpea flour), buckwheat flour, bajra or almond flour with wheat flour for protein-rich chapatis.
6. Milk Matters: Consider having milk daily and consider adding extra to tea (opt for semi-skimmed milk if you have high cholesterol). Incorporate cheese in your diet, there are many varieties from paneer, feta, edam, cheddar, halloumi etc. With Edam cheese containing the most protein. Moderation is key for those with high cholesterol and Apetina paneer is a good choice as it contains less fat than regular paneer.

Note for People with Diabetes: Be cautious with protein bars and shakes, as they often contain high sugar content. Fresh, whole-food protein sources are a better choice. Remember, a balanced diet that includes adequate protein contributes to overall health and well-being.

Foods containing all 9 essential amino acids	**Foods that contain some essential amino acids:**
Milk Cheese Yogurt Tofu/Soya Quinoa Chia Seeds Fish Egg Meat	Nuts Seeds Grains Fruit Vegetables Beans Legumes

For vegetarians, a variety of plant-based and dairy proteins are key to ensure you are getting all 9 essential amino acids from your diet so try to opt for at least one food from the essential amino acid list foods per meal.

Some examples of complete protein-based vegetarian meals:

- Dal with rice and quinoa
- Chapati with dal and yogurt
- Chapati with sabzi and yogurt
- Paneer with rice or chapati
- Tofu stir fry
- Adding chia seeds to your morning porridge
- Quinoa salad

FATS

Previously mentioned, fats play a crucial role in our bodies. However, excessive consumption of fats, particularly harmful ones, increases the risk of high cholesterol, which is associated with various cardiovascular complications. There are two primary types of fats to reduce in your diet:

Saturated fats: Limit your intake of these fats, as they are more likely to clog your arteries, especially if you're physically inactive. Saturated fats are found in fried foods (such as chips, crisps, samosas, and pakoras), red meat, full-fat dairy products (like milk, butter, and ghee), burgers, and various snacks (cakes, biscuits, chocolates, and mithai).

Trans fats: Avoid these altogether! Trans fats are another harmful type of fat. They are created by heating unsaturated fats and oils at very high temperatures, often to extend the shelf life of processed foods. You'll find trans fats in items like cakes, frozen pizzas, biscuits, fried foods, takeaway meals, and margarine. For instance, vegetable oil can be converted into solid margarine through this process. If you come across terms like 'hydrogenated fats' or 'mono or diglycerides of fatty acids' in food ingredients, steer clear, as these indicate high trans fat content. Excessive consumption of trans fats can elevate LDL (bad) cholesterol levels and lead to artery blockages. If you still crave these foods, consider cooking them at home using fresh ingredients, opting for oven-baked homemade chips, making burgers and pizzas from scratch, or choosing healthier alternatives like baked crisps.

In our diet, we should incorporate healthier fats over unhealthier fats.

Unsaturated fats: Opt for unsaturated fats when consuming fatty foods or cooking with fats. These fats have health benefits, as they help reduce bad cholesterol levels in our bodies. Sources of unsaturated fats include nuts, seeds, avocado, and oily fish like salmon, which also provide omega-3 fatty acids that support heart health.

During the winter months, many of us prepare traditional dishes like 'pinniya' or 'panjeeri.' Winter is a time when we need to conserve energy to stay warm. These dishes typically contain nuts and seeds, which contribute to our overall health by providing good fats. While our grandparents made these recipes with ingredients like atta (whole wheat flour), ghee, and sugar, it's essential to adapt them to our modern lifestyle. These ancient recipes should be retained but adapted to our lifestyle today. Have a look in the recipe section for a healthy panjeeri recipe.

FRUIT

Many individuals with Diabetes may hesitate to eat fruits, fearing an impact on their blood sugar. However, choosing fruit as a snack is a healthier option than indulging in sweets like mithai. Fruits generally have a lower glycaemic index, meaning they won't cause blood sugar levels to spike as rapidly as sugary desserts like cake. It's perfectly fine for those with Diabetes to enjoy fruits, which offer a wealth of minerals and vitamins crucial for health. It's important to monitor portion sizes—aim for no more than five servings of fruit per day, with one serving being about the size of your palm. Opt for fresh fruits, be sparing with dried fruits, and steer clear of canned fruits, which often have added sugars for preservation.

Consuming whole fruits is preferable to drinking fruit juices or smoothies. Juicing can lead to a higher release of sugars and the loss of fibre, especially if the peel is removed. Fibre plays a vital role in gut health and in moderating the natural sugars in fruits, leading to a more gradual sugar release. It also helps reduce the risk of heart disease. If you're a fan of juice, go for pure, unsweetened varieties and practice portion control by limiting yourself to a small 150ml serving rather than a full glass. Be mindful that some fruits have higher sugar content than others; for instance, an overripe banana will elevate blood sugar levels more swiftly than one that's not fully ripe.

DRINKS

Our bodies are approximately 60% water, underscoring the importance of hydration for cellular function. It's recommended to drink 6-8 glasses of water per day, with each glass being about 200ml, unless you're on a fluid-restricted diet. While some may find it challenging to consume this volume of water, integrating it into your daily routine can help establish a habit. Ayurvedic traditions suggest drinking a glass of warm water upon waking to rehydrate and detoxify after approximately 8 hours without water during sleep. A simple indicator of hydration is urine colour; dark yellow urine often signals dehydration, prompting a need to increase water intake.

There's no need to consume all your daily water at once. Instead, sip it gradually throughout the day, allowing at least 30 minutes after eating before drinking to let digestive enzymes work effectively; immediate drinking can dilute these enzymes and slow digestion.

For those accustomed to sugary beverages like juice, soda, or squash, consider switching to water flavoured with a slice of fruit. If you're reducing fizzy drink consumption, sparkling water is a good alternative. Tea and coffee contribute to your water intake, but it's best to minimize added sugars. Be mindful that excessive caffeine can lead to dehydration, decreased mineral absorption, and potentially increased blood pressure.

Try swapping for hot water, herbal teas or decaffeinated drinks. Drinking water also helps to reduce water retention, as the more salt we have in our body the more our body tries to dilute this by holding onto water – resulting in water retention which is often accompanied with bloating.

JUNK FOODS

Indulging in a packet of crisps or a chocolate bar can be a delightful treat, provided it's done sparingly and not as part of our daily routine. These snacks are typically laden with fats, salts, sugars, artificial preservatives, and processed components that can negatively impact our health. Their addictive nature stems from the release of dopamine they trigger, which brings about a sense of pleasure. Consequently, we may find ourselves craving these foods more frequently, eventually requiring larger quantities to achieve the same level of satisfaction.

The challenge some individuals face in curbing their consumption of these foods isn't a matter of willpower; it's a physiological response to the addictive qualities of the ingredients. If you find yourself habitually reaching for junk food, consider gradually reducing your intake rather than quitting cold turkey, which could intensify cravings and lead to a relapse into old habits. Sugar, much like nicotine, has addictive properties—the more we consume, the more we desire. Starting the day with a sugary breakfast can set the stage for sugar cravings throughout the day. Reducing sugar intake can be a gradual process, and sudden cessation might lead to withdrawal symptoms like headaches for those accustomed to high sugar levels. Enjoying cakes, biscuits, or mithai with tea is a pleasure many share, but it's healthier to reserve such treats for special occasions rather than daily indulgence.

A practical approach to avoid overconsumption is to refrain from purchasing these items during your grocery runs. If they aren't readily available at home, you're less likely to eat them. Consider opting for smaller or individual-sized packages to help control portions. For those who enjoy mithai or cake, homemade versions using natural ingredients allow for better control over sugar content and offer an opportunity to explore different flavours. It's also an excellent way to involve children in the cooking process and instil healthy eating habits .I have found snacks for babies and toddlers are generally healthier as their biscuits and crisps often contain no added sugar but are sweetened naturally from fruit and are generally less processed. These could be an idea if you are craving a sweet or savoury snack but wanted something heathier, there's no reason as to why adults or older children can't consume them.

Remember, moderation is key, and making small, sustainable changes can lead to a healthier lifestyle.

PROCESSED FOODS

Processed foods are altered from their original state into new forms, ranging from the conversion of solid foods into powders for meal replacement shakes to the creation of flour from wheat or vegetarian burgers from pea proteins. The extent of processing varies; not all processed foods are detrimental—for instance, using flour to make fresh chapati is minimal processing. However, more complex processing, like that used to produce frozen pizza, involves additional steps, preservatives and additives.

Ready meals and other processed foods often contain high levels of salts, fats, sugars, additives, and preservatives to extend their shelf life. These are ultra processed foods. Frequent consumption of these highly processed items has been associated with various health issues, including certain cancers, Type 2 Diabetes, Dementia, and heart disease. These foods have become staples in our fast-paced lives, often at the expense of our well-being.

Preparing meals with fresh ingredients, as opposed to relying on pre-packaged options, can significantly benefit your health. It can lead to improvements in weight, skin condition, blood glucose, and cholesterol levels, and may even boost fertility. For effective Diabetes management, it's crucial to limit the intake of heavily processed foods. When shopping, scrutinize the level of processing and the ingredients list. Unfamiliar ingredients are likely artificial additives, especially those with added E numbers. Research these ingredients online to understand their potential health impacts. Quite often we reward children with these foods - giving them a chocolate or sweet as a treat. Sadly we are fuelling their taste for these processed food.

The most ultra processed food that we eat in the UK is factory produced bread. We opt for wholemeal as its healthier, (it is in the sense as its wholegrain) but still there are multiple added ingredients from palm oils to trans fats, sugar, high levels of salt as well as many additives to prolong the shelf life. I have began to make my own bread now and regret not making it sooner as its so easy to prepare and contains no preservatives. We often have a piece of bread or a wrap instead of chapati believing that its lighter and healthier when in actual fact, the homemade chapati contains only two ingredients - water and flour in comparison to the multiple ingredients in bread.

To understand your dependence on processed foods, try spending a day without them and observe how you feel without them. You can find contact details at the back of the book to share your experience.

Regular excessive consumption of alcohol has been associated with a higher risk of developing Type 2 Diabetes. For some Diabetics, it is ok to consume alcohol in moderation but make sure it is not exceeding the government guidelines of 14 units a week [20].

What is 1 unit of alcohol (average amounts)?

- A pint of beer - **2.3 units**
- A bottle of beer - **1.7 units**
- A 175ml glass of wine - **2.3 units**
- A 125ml Champagne glass - **1.5 units**
- A single 25ml measure of a spirit is - **1 unit**

Cocktails will contain various units, as often they are a mixture of different alcohols.

Today, there's an extensive variety of alcoholic drinks available, each varying in sugar content and carbohydrate levels. When considering your sugar levels, it's essential to read the nutritional information on the back of the drink. For individuals with diabetes, opting for beverages with the lowest sugar and carbohydrate content is advisable. Keep in mind that even drinks low in sugar and carbs can contribute to overall calorie intake, potentially leading to weight gain and an increased risk of Type 2 Diabetes.
Cocktails often contain significant amounts of sugar, and liqueurs are also high in sugar content. When mixing spirits, be mindful of the mixer you choose. For example, the popular combination of rum and Coke should be evaluated in terms of sugar content. Additionally, snacks like fried peanuts, Bombay mix, and crisps frequently accompany alcoholic drinks. These snacks add to the overall calorie count due to their high fat and carbohydrate content.

Now, let's discuss alcohol's impact on diabetes complications. Alcohol affects the liver, which stores excess glucose as glycogen. Individuals taking insulin or sulfonylurea medications are at a higher risk of hypoglycemia (hypos). When blood sugar levels drop, the liver may not efficiently convert glycogen into glucose for the body to use, potentially impairing hypo symptoms. Severe hypos can be life-threatening. If you're on these medications, limit alcohol consumption, and if you choose to drink, pair it with food containing complex carbohydrates to prevent hypos.

Alcohol and Peer Pressure

Alcohol is often free-flowing at any desi functions, especially desi parties, making it easier to give in to temptation. Many of us can probably relate to feeling pressured into having alcohol in this type of environment as people tell you to have just one more drink and before you know it, you have had a few pints and a couple of shots.

I'm sure we all know that one person who has a target to finish a bottle of whiskey like it's a heroic achievement, and if you end up at a table with this person, you will get pressurised all evening. Before giving into this type of pressure, try taking a step back and think whether putting someone's demands before your health is worth it. At the end of the day it is you and your family that will have to deal with you becoming ill, not the person who pressurised you to have those extra drinks.

SAUCES

Many sauces also contain sugar, which is often used to preserve the sauces and enhance the flavours. A famous tamarind sauce has two teaspoons of sugar per tablespoon of sauce! One spoon of some BBQ sauces contains one spoon of sugar, similar to the sugar in a spoon of tomato ketchup. Please be aware of the sugar content when using these sauces, especially when controlling your glucose levels.

Nowadays, we use many ready-made cooking sauces to help with our cooking chores. Life has become so busy that we often buy these things for convenience. Many of these sauces contain sugar, from a jar of pasta sauce containing six spoons of sugar to a jar of butter chicken sauce containing five and a half spoons of sugar! Eventually, all the sugars add up and before we realise we have exceeded the maximum recommended daily allowance of 7 spoons of sugar. Instead of using ready-made cooking sauces, make your own at home. This way, you are not only eating fresh, but you will also know what has precisely gone into your foods. It's also a great way to reduce our sugar intake. In addition, cooking yourself is a great way to keep active and a way to get creative with creating sauces from different ingredients.

FOOD TRAFFIC LIGHT LABELING

Many foods have the food traffic light labelling system on the front of the foods packaging. This is a great guide to do a quick check to see how healthy the foods are. It's a colour-coded system that shows whether the food contains high, medium, or low amounts of fat, salt, and sugars [21]. Using this guide is a great way to select foods when we are doing our food shopping. It also gives us information on what percentage of our daily intake of fats, sugars and salts are in a serving of that particular food.

Red means the food/drink contains a high amount of a certain type of ingredient that can be bad for health and these food should not be consumed regular

Amber means medium amount of ingredient that is bad to health. This colour indicates you can eat it most of the time.

Green means low amount of bad ingredients. If there are more green lights on the label this means the food is healthy to consume.

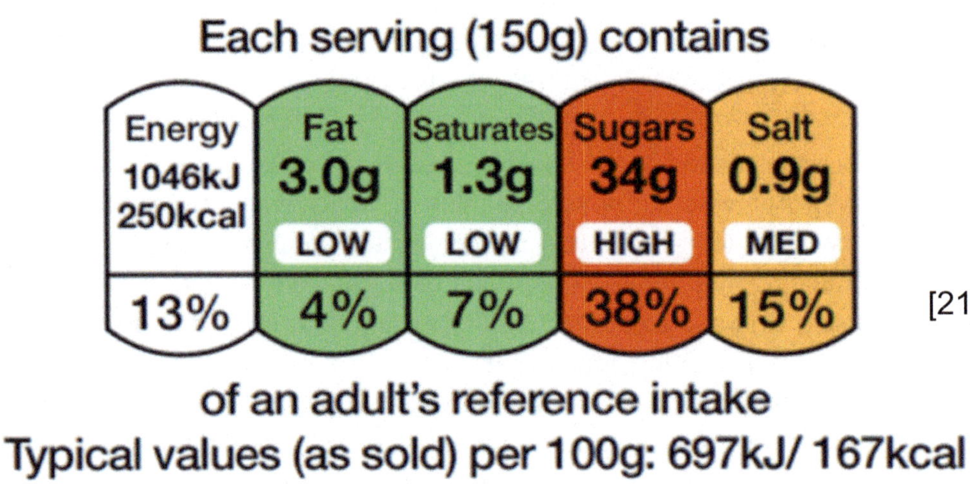

[21]

FAMILY FUNCTIONS AND DIABETES

South Asian gatherings often feature indulgent foods, from fried aloo tikki to rich ras malai. Weddings, in particular, can span an entire week of feasting. However, if you're diabetic or aiming for a healthier diet, navigating these food-filled events can be challenging. So, how can we maintain a balanced approach in such an environment?

1. Starters and Portion Control - Exercise portion control. You don't need to sample everything on the menu; leave room for the main course. Opt for better choices. For instance, choose an aloo tikki over a samosa. A samosa contains double the carbohydrates found in potatoes and wheat, while an aloo tikki is primarily made from potatoes. Pair starters with salads to balance flavour's and nutrition.
2. Main Course - Approach the main course as you would at home, similar portions. Be mindful of carbohydrates. Avoid consuming rice and roti (bread) together. If naan is on the menu, have half the portion you would for roti, as naans typically contain double the carbohydrates.
3. Alcohol Considerations - Alcoholic beverages are often abundant at such events. Moderation is key; the choice of how much to drink is in your hands.
4. Dessert Decisions - If it's been a while since you enjoyed something sweet, go ahead and savour a dessert. However, if you've already had a week's worth of sweet treats, consider sharing with someone or skipping dessert altogether.

Participating in South Asian dinners with family and friends often involves bringing a gift to the host's house. Typically, these gifts take the form of mithai (sweets), chocolates, or biscuits. Upon arrival, we're often greeted with a sugary welcome drink either a fizzy beverage or juice. However, we have the option to choose water instead if we prefer.

During these get-togethers, which usually span a few hours of socializing and feasting, portion control becomes crucial. Hosts sometimes serve generous portions, and before we realize it, we've indulged in starters, mains, and desserts. It's essential to recognize that everyone's portion size varies, and we should respect individual preferences.

I recall when I first got married; my in-laws mistook my portion control for shyness at the dinner table. However, it was merely the amount I was accustomed to eating. During such gatherings, there's nothing wrong with politely informing the host about your desired portion or putting food on your plate yourself. Advocating for your health is essential because if you don't speak up, no one else will.

Similarly, when hosting others, consider their health conditions and avoid force-feeding. Some people may take offense if you decline sweet offerings, especially during 'mu mitha' (celebratory moments involving sweets). In such situations, confidently decline or have a small portion, explaining your health concerns. Most people will respect your choices.

When my husband and I go over to my mums, she says she has brought my husband's favourite biscuits, which makes him give into eating the biscuits. These cheeky mums will try anything to feed us!

PORTION SIZE

Extensive research has linked plastics to various health issues, including fertility problems. Plastic containers are commonly used for take-out foods, but when we put hot foods in these containers, plastic particles can leach into the food. Some of us even rely on plastic dishes for reheating and eating meals. However, what are the long-term health implications of using plastic, and why should we consider alternatives like stainless steel? Our ancestors often used stainless steel dishes, and there are compelling reasons to follow their lead. Unlike plastic, stainless steel containers are made of non-toxic materials and do not release harmful chemicals into our food. Let's explore this further.

One traditional South Asian dish that exemplifies portion control is the humble 'thali' Many households have these dishes, often tucked away and gathering dust. However, they serve as an excellent example of how our elders managed portion sizes. The taal features separate compartments for chapati, salad, yogurt, dal, and sabzi. Notably, these compartments are not very deep, allowing us to regulate the amount of food we consume. Now, let's compare this to our modern dinner plates and bowls. Take a closer look at their size and depth. Often, we pile various foods onto these larger dishes without considering portion control. By contrast, the taal encourages mindful eating. Sometimes, the bigger the dish, the more tempted we are to overfill it. Perhaps it's time to embrace the wisdom of our ancestors and opt for healthier alternatives like stainless steel.

Another great way to portion control is by using our palm as a guide, roughly having a palm size serving of fruit is a portion (see next page). If you are trying to lose weight, have a look at the dishes you are using and maybe consider making a change. Bring out the thali when having South Asian foods to help with portion control, also using it means fewer dishes to wash as we're not using multiple plates. In this same way look at the glasses you have for your drinks, what size are they? Did you know a recommended portion of juice is 150ml, not a pint of juice that we are often served in restaurants. The same applies to fizzy drinks.

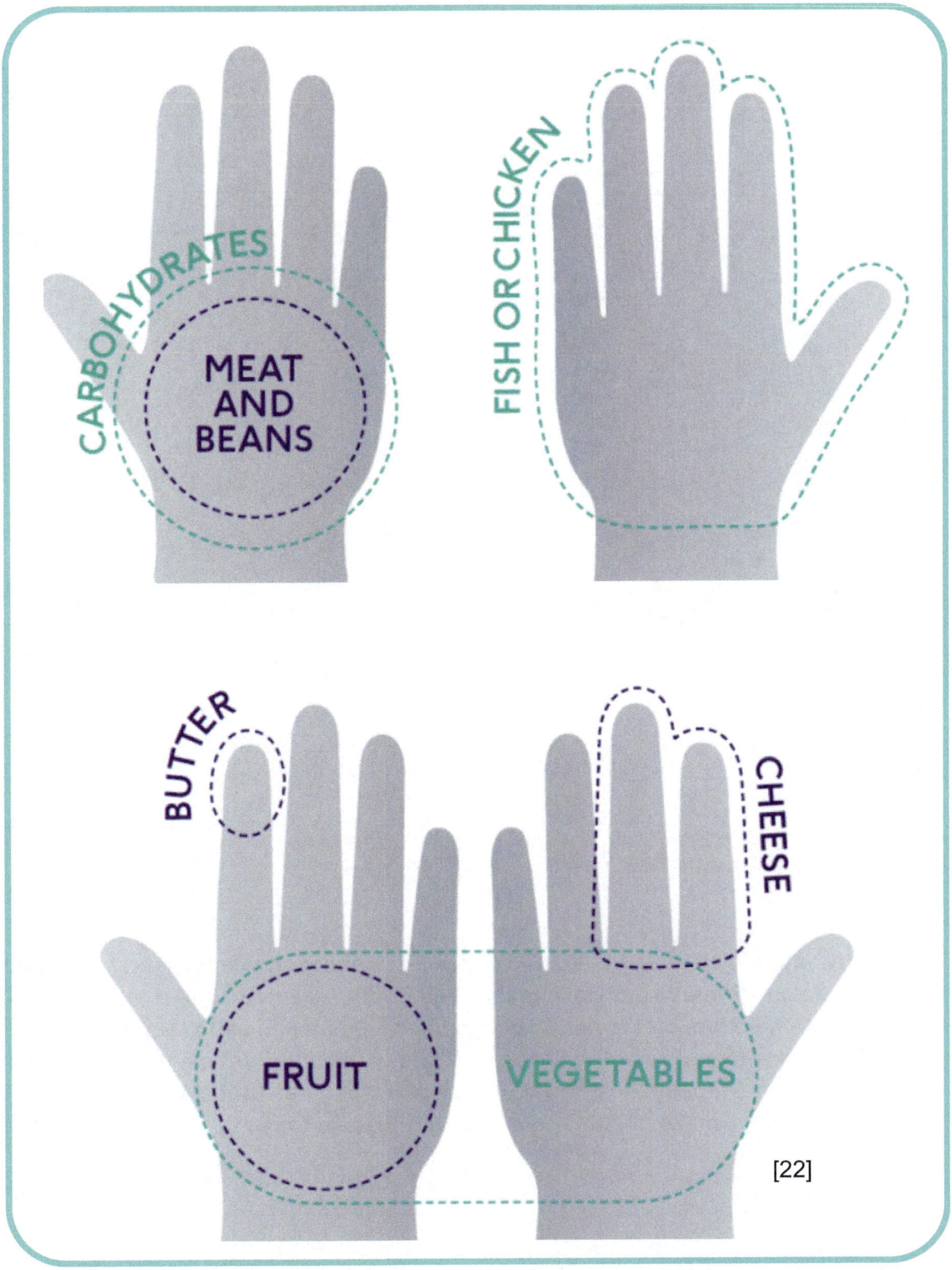

This is a great tool provided by the British Heart Foundation. It provides us with a guide of what portion size we should be having of the different food groups. Using this is ideal for those looking to lose weight or generally looking to eat healthier. How does your portion of these foods match up to these examples?

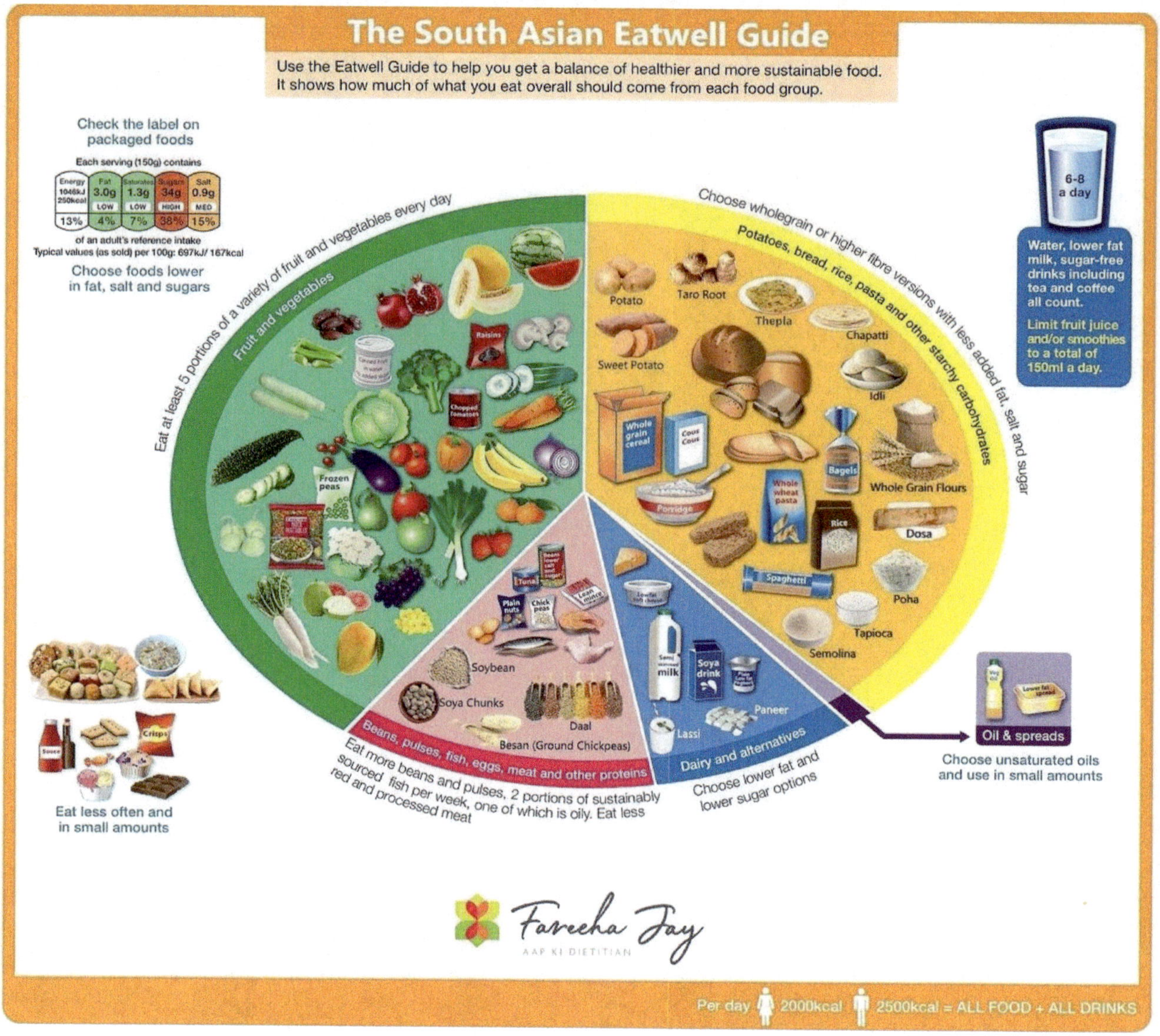

[23]

The healthy eating plate that we are use to seeing is aimed at Western diets. A South Asian Dietician - Fareeha Jay has created this South Asian version of the healthy eating plate to help reduce the health inequalities when it comes to Desi foods. You can use this plate to see what Desi foods fall into which food groups and use it as a guide to help you choose the correct portion sizes of these foods. Helping you to make healthier choices during meal times.

SWEETENERS

Artificial sweeteners have become popular alternatives to sugar due to their lower or zero calorie content. Commonly used sweeteners include acesulfame, aspartame, erythritol, saccharin, sorbitol, steviol glycosides, sucralose, and xylitol. These additives find their way into our diets through various avenues: added to teas and coffees instead of sugar, present in 'low-sugar' drinks, and even incorporated into sweets, foods, and toothpaste.
The marketing strategy often touts these products as 'low sugar,' leading consumers to assume they are healthier choices. However, it's essential to recognize that artificial sweeteners are synthetic chemicals designed to mimic the familiar sweet taste.

Despite their popularity, artificial sweeteners can have side effects when consumed excessively. These may include stomach upset, bloating, and a laxative effect. Recently, the World Health Organization (WHO) classified aspartame (a commonly used sweetener) as 'possibly carcinogenic to humans' , indicating a potential link to cancer [24]. Aspartame is found in various foods and drinks, including Diet Coke (check your low-sugar products at home to see if they contain it).

Given the potential risks associated with excessive sweetener consumption, it's reasonable to consider that a small amount of natural sugar might be safer than relying heavily on artificial sweeteners. Remember, the more artificial substances we consume, the greater the impact on our health. Opting for a natural, minimally processed diet remains the best choice for overall well-being.

DIET PILLS

When it comes to dieting many of us want a quick fix to lose weight as fast as possible. Some people turn to diet pills which magically helps to reduce weight. One common diet pill works by preventing the absorption of the fat that we have in our diet, instead this fat is excreted in our poo. A common side effect of these pills is diarrhoea as well as low Vitamin D levels as Vitamin D is a fat-soluble vitamin. Would it not make more sense to eat less fat to begin with? It's much safer for us to have a healthier balanced diet accompanied with regular physical activity than taking dieting pills.

FASTING & DIABETES

Fasting is a common practice in many South Asian communities, taking various forms. From complete abstinence from food and water during religious observances like Karva Chauth in Hinduism and Ramadan in Islam to dietary restrictions during Navratri, fasting holds both cultural and health significance as it allows the digestive system to rest, which aids with detoxing the body. Even in the Western world, intermittent fasting has gained popularity.

However, for diabetic patients, especially those on insulin or sulfonylurea medications fasting can pose risks. It may significantly reduce blood sugar levels, leading to hypoglycaemia with serious complications. Some fasts involve avoiding specific foods, such as salt. For individuals taking diuretic medications for blood pressure, this can be problematic because diuretics increase salt and water removal, potentially resulting in dangerously low salt levels. Thankfully, many cultural traditions allow exemptions for specific groups, including children, pregnant individuals, the elderly, and those with health conditions. If you have diabetes, please do not force yourself to fast. Instead, consider alternative ways to observe the occasion. You might choose to give up sugary or fried foods, quit smoking, engage in charity work, or allocate more time for prayers.

Before embarking on any fasting regimen, consult your healthcare team. They can assess your health, review your medications, and provide personalized advice on whether fasting is safe for you.

Remember, your health always comes first, and there are various ways to participate in cultural and religious practices without compromising your well-being.

HERBAL REMEDIES

Some people turn to herbal remedies to help control their sugar levels. I often hear people talk about karela (bitter gourd) and methi (fenugreek) seeds to help lower glucose levels. There has been some research showing that both foods may aid in lowering glucose levels [25,26]. If you are considering any herbal preparations, it's important to continue your prescribed medication as normal and let your healthcare professional know before you start taking any herbal preparation as there may be interactions between the herbs and your medication. As with all herbal preparation please ensure you are purchasing it from a reputable company with someone who can give you qualified advice on the herbs. Never purchase anything online from random websites and never take without consulting a medical practioner.

06

COOKING

MAKING DESI FOOD HEALTHIER

Enjoying desi foods doesn't equate to an unhealthy diet. In fact, Indian cuisine offers numerous health benefits, especially due to the rich array of spices we incorporate. Let's explore some of these advantages:

- Turmeric (Haldi): Known for its anti-inflammatory properties, turmeric is a staple spice in Indian cooking. It supports overall health and may help reduce inflammation.
- Cumin (Jeera): Cumin acts as an antioxidant, aiding in neutralizing harmful free radicals and contains iron
- Ginger: A powerhouse for digestion, ginger soothes the stomach and promotes gut health. It's a common ingredient in Indian curries and teas.
- Garlic: Besides adding flavour, garlic is believed to strengthen the immune system. It's used generously in Indian cooking.
- Lentils (Dals): Lentils are rich in fibre, supporting heart health and digestive function. They also provide essential nutrients like folate, iron, and protein.
- Yogurt (Dahi): A probiotic superstar, yogurt aids healthy digestion and provides protein and calcium. It's a frequent accompaniment to Desi meals.

Additionally, many Desi households prepare these foods fresh—from sabzi to dal to piping-hot chapatis. Speaking of chapatis, they are the Desi staple bread, akin to the diverse breads found in other cultures. Contrary to processed breads, wraps, and buns from stores, chapatis are healthier. Why?

- Freshness: Chapatis are made fresh without added preservatives.
- Nutritional Benefits: Freshly prepared foods retain more nutrients than heavily processed alternatives.

Rather than eliminating these wholesome foods, focus on portion control and adapt your cooking practices to your current lifestyle. By doing so, you can reduce the risk of diabetes and its complications while savouring the flavours of Desi cuisine. Remember, balance and mindful choices are key to maintaining health while enjoying the foods we love.

Here are some tips for making our Desi food healthier:

Chapatis

- Prepare the atta fresh, with enough atta for how many chapatis everyone is going to eat, this reduces wastage as well as overeating as you're only preparing how much you need

- Have a maximum of 1-2 roti's per meal (dependent on how big the chapati is – if its big have one if it's small then have a maximum of two) this gives us enough carbohydrates. If you are hungrier opt for having more dal, yogurt or sabzi instead of reaching for another chapati, as there's more protein in dal and yogurt than in a chapati, keeping you fuller for longer.

- Using wholemeal atta (if you find it too dry – try wholemeal chakki atta which has been finely ground to give the softest roti)

- Multigrain atta is another great alternative as it has a variety of grains and delivers a range of nutrients to our diet through the mixture of grains it contain. It also has a lower glycaemic index than white atta

- Keep the pehra (dough for each chapati) small – the smaller the pehra the smaller the size of carbohydrates we are having

- Ask everyone how many chapatis they want to prevent making extra as we are more likely to eat the leftovers and end up overeating. If there are any leftovers, have them the next day as a wrap with the leftover sabzi. We eat wraps that have an expiry date for the following year, we don't know how long ago these were prepared, or what preservatives have been added, but we're not willing to have a roti that was prepared the day before

- If cholesterol levels are raised avoid buttering the chapati with ghee or butter, instead have it dry

- Avoid having rice when having chapati as this adds up to two carbohydrates

- Try different grains such as bajra, jowar, ragi, maki, oat, chickpea flour for making chapatis as it diversifies our wholegrain intake, increases fibre intake and can contain more protein. You could mix these flours with your normal atta too.

Paratha's

In many households, it's tradition to have Parathas on a Sunday, with the classic favourite being aloo parathas. But did you know an average aloo paratha breaks down into the equivalent effect of **6 spoons of sugar** once digested, possibly, even more, depending on how much aloo and atta has been used to prepare them. Try to reduce the carbohydrate content of parathas by using vegetables instead of aloo. Try swapping for broccoli, spinach, mooli, beetroot, or any other vegetables in the fridge. A great one to try in the summer is mint and ajwain, as mint has a cooling effect on the body, and ajwain is excellent for digestion. Instead of making a paratha with the filling between two parathas, add the filling into the atta when preparing it. For example, add finely chopped spinach into the atta and mix instead of putting it into the middle of two parathas, as this again doubles our carbohydrate content.

Also, paratha doesn't have to be made in butter, try using rapeseed oil instead, or if your cholesterol is high, you don't need oil or butter to cook it. It will be like a tandoori paratha or kulcha, and how good do they taste! You can have it as a filled roti instead cooked with no butter or oil but the same great filling. If you are going to treat yourself to a few aloo parathas, then try to ensure you are extra active that day so that you burn off the excess carbohydrates, go for a nice long walk afterwards so that the extra glucose isn't getting stored.

Sabzi

Many of our sabzi's are made using vegetables, and a lot of sabzi's are made by adding aloo – aloo matar, aloo gobi, aloo falia, aloo baingan. Vegetables already contain some carbohydrates, and adding potatoes increases the carbohydrate load. When we have this type of sabzi with chapati or rice, we are doubling our carbohydrates (remember to stick to one carbohydrate per meal instead). So, for such sabzi's, try reducing the amount of potato you put in or cutting out the potato altogether, such as having gajar matter instead of aloo gajar or try gobi with cashews. Get experimenting in the kitchen. When cooking the sabzi, use only a teaspoon of oil for the tadka to lower cholesterol intake. When making sabzi, make enough to last two days. That way, you can have the leftovers for lunch or dinner the next day. When making paneer, try to add more vegetables to the sabzi, as paneer often contains a lot of fat. By adding vegetables, we are balancing out the fat in the sabzi. Palak paneer is an excellent sabzi as it includes lots of fresh spinach. Chilli paneer can be made by adding lots of peppers, mangetout, and sugar snaps as the vegetables give it that great crunch.
Keeping frozen vegetables in is a great aid when making a quick sabzi after work, as frozen vegetables still contain lots of vitamins and minerals as they are often frozen on the day they were picked to maintain the freshness of the vegetables. These can easily be added to any sabzi.

Oil

Oil forms the basis of many of our South Asian dishes. The amount of oil used for foods varies from house to house. I'm sure we have all had dinner at someone's home, and their dishes have a lot of oil floating on top! When doing a tadka, all we need is a tablespoon of oil. A lot of oils that desi foods are cooked with are refined oils. These are often the big bottle of oil you can purchase from the desi stores. These oils have been chemically changed, often using a bleaching process to make the oil lighter in colour and convert healthy fats into trans fat due to high-temperature processing. This also alters the smell of the oil if you think about pure mustard oil and its strong aroma, compared to the neutral scent of refined oils. Trans fats can clog the arteries and are linked to some cancers and heart disease. It is better to use cold-pressed oils instead. As the name suggests, the oils are extracted using a cold process, thus not heated, so it does not chemically alter the oil. When selecting a cooking oil, opt for a cold-pressed oil instead.

There are two types of fats we need to look at when selecting our cooking oil, saturated and unsaturated fats. Saturated fats can cause health problems if consumed regularly, especially with an inactive lifestyle. These are present in refined cooking oils, lard, butter, and ghee, leading to high cholesterol and heart disease. On the other hand, unsaturated fats such as those found in rapeseed oil, sunflower oil, and olive oil help to combat the bad fats helping to reduce our cholesterol levels.

Some people reuse the oil they use to fry foods multiple times. This can cause more harm than good in the long run. I have heard a few people say the more the oil has been reused, the better it is! This needs to be corrected. For example, when frying samosa, the oil used should be left to cool and disposed of according to local guidelines. When that oil is reused repeatedly, the excess heat makes the fats burn, forming aldehydes that are harmful and regular consumption is linked to certain cancers and heart disease.

Every oil has a different smoke point – the temperature at which it begins to smoke and loses its nutritional properties. It is essential to use the correct oil with the right smoke point for cooking; for example, when deep frying or doing a tadka at high heat, you must use an oil with a high smoke point. A good choice for this type of oil would be rapeseed oil or sunflower oil. On the other hand, olive oil has a lower smoke point, so it shouldn't be used for this type of cooking. Instead, use it for salads instead or cooking with a low flame.

Some low-calorie oil sprays that people use often contain additional chemicals that may do more harm than good at high heat. Using a small quantity of pure oil instead of oil sprays is better.

When doing a tadka, if the heat is too much, the tadka may start to burn. You can add a little water instead of more oil to continue cooking.

CHAI TIME

When having guests over we always make sure they are well fed. Even if they pop over for a cup of chai, this must be accompanied by some type of food. Usually what we put out with chai is often fried foods, from samosa,s, and pakora's to spring rolls, bread pakora, paneer pakora to aloo tikki. But who said starters have to be fried? There are other healthier ways to cook these foods. We all have ovens these days, if we don't have time to prepare samosas or spring rolls from scratch then you could always purchase them uncooked from your local desi shop and cook them in the oven yourself to reduce the fat content. Serve a nice salad with the food so you are balancing out the meal (check out the recipe section for more ideas). Aloo chaat and sweet potato chaats are other great alternatives for starters. Again, you could always serve something totally different instead of the norm, maybe opt for pitta bread cut in strips with hummus or an afternoon tea style small sandwiches, a fruit platter or fruit chaat in the summer months, bhel puri with added nuts and seeds. The ideas are endless, you just need to go with your creativity in the kitchen.

Whilst making desi chai, always make it using loose tea leaves as many tea bags contain plastic which are not designed to be boiled. When making tea for everyone make it without sugar, what we tend to do is put in a load of sugar without measuring it, instead, make it without sugar, and then everyone can add in the amount that they need. If your trying to stop having sugar in tea, flavour with cinnamon, fennel seeds or cardamom to give you different flavours. Usually with chai we also put out something sweet like mithai, cakes, and biscuits, you could swap this for nuts instead, roasted dal/chana or homemade steamed dhokla.

TIPS FOR COOKING

- Try to cook healthy meals at home instead of opting for take outs and ready meals.

- Prepare in advance, the basis of many South Asian cooking is ginger, garlic and chilli's we can prep in advance by cutting and blending this beforehand and freezing until we are ready to cook with them.

- Stock up on dry goods such as wholewheat pasta, brown rice, dal's, they have long dates and are great pantry fillers ready to use for meals when needed.

- Stock up on frozen vegetables these are washed and cut ready for use when needed especially good midweek when there's no time pop into the shops these are great as a side dish and to be added to meals such as pasta.

- Prepare for the next day - when cooking evening meals try to make double so that you have enough for lunch the next day, this is great for those going into work as it prevents them dashing out at lunchtime to get a takeout. For those that don't have a microwave at work invest in a thermal flask - heat your lunch at home before heading to work, place in a flask and it should remain warm for lunchtime.

- Try to cook with different whole grains as the more grains we have in our diet the more beneficial for our health as they all contain different vitamins, fibre, and minerals. Sometimes we find ourselves eating a lot of wheat - toast for breakfast, sandwiches for lunch, and chapati for the evening. But there are so many other grains we could try like oats for breakfast, quinoa for lunch, and brown rice for the evening. This way we are getting more fibre in our diet and a great variety of nutrients.

- Eat as many vegetables as possible, opt for a rainbow of vegetables as the more coloured fruit or vegetables we have the more vitamins and minerals we will be getting into our cells. Red peppers have a good amount of Vitamin C, carrots are high in Vitamin A, and cauliflowers contain choline which helps with memory, the more variety of vegetables we eat the more health benefits we will receive. Vegetables are great for a side dish, as a sabzi, or put into a main dish such as stir-fried noodles with vegetables.

- Get the whole family involved in healthy cooking, try a new recipe each week, with a variety of ingredients, who knows you may release your inner cook or find your new family favourite. Nowadays with the internet, there are so many ways to access so many free recipe ideas which can be adapted to the ingredients you currently have at home

- Soak dals the night before to get rid of any impurities as well as making the dal quicker to cook

- Brown rice often takes a while to cook so reduce the cooking time by pre soaking the rice

- Eat less processed foods by purchasing less of these foods when you are food shopping

- Buy more fresh fruits and vegetables and aim to eat at least 5 portions a day

- Try to buy less sugary foods for the children and incorporate healthy home made snacks into their diet instead

- Buy less fizzy and sugary drinks. Instead make your own flavoured water using fresh fruits

- Try not to overcook the vegetables, sometimes when cooking sabzis we tend to overcook them, and this reduces the amount of nutrients we gain from them. So, when cooking vegetables stop the flame once they are cooked, aim to cook them so they still retain their natural bright colour

- Add a dash of lime or lemon to sabzi's as they contain Vitamin C and will improve iron absorption from the food

HEALTHY MEALS

Some individuals believe that skipping meals will accelerate their weight loss goals. However, often when we skip meals, we end up snacking impulsively—usually on quick, convenient junk food. To maintain a healthier approach, consider having three balanced meals each day. This practice helps prevent excessive snacking and keeps us satiated for longer periods.

Now, let's delve into the science behind meal frequency and insulin:

1. Meal Frequency and Insulin Activation - The more frequently we eat, the more our pancreas releases insulin. Insulin plays a crucial role in regulating blood sugar levels. However, consistent insulin spikes can lead to insulin resistance, especially when we consume refined carbohydrates during meals and processed snacks in between.
2. Smart Sweet Treats - On days when you indulge in something sweet, have it directly after a meal. Why? Because the fats and proteins in the meal help stabilize the sugar release from the sweet treat. This approach prevents a sharp rise in glucose levels and avoids another insulin surge a few hours later.
3. Building a Balanced Meal - A well-rounded meal should include, small amount of healthy fats, adequate protein, unrefined complex carbohydrate (such as whole grains) and plenty of vegetables
4. Colourful Fruits and Vegetables - Aim for a rainbow of fruits and veggies. Each colour provides a unique set of vitamins and minerals. For instance orange vegetables (like carrots and pumpkin) contain beta carotene, essential for healthy eyes.

Breakfast

Breakfast is one of the most important meals of the day as it's when we break the fast, hence the name breakfast. In many Desi households, it's tradition to start the day with tea and biscuits (not sure where this tradition started), but this is one of the worst things you could have for breakfast. Breakfast sets us up for the day ahead; therefore, it should be hearty and healthy, with good fats, complex carbohydrates, and protein. A good breakfast will keep us going until lunchtime and should stop the need for snacking. If we start with biscuits and eat breakfast later, we increase our glucose levels twice. It's better to have breakfast followed by a cup of tea instead. Many people opt for cereal for breakfast as it's quick and easy, but these can be heavily processed. The least processed I have come across is shredded wheat, which contains just whole wheat in the ingredients. Aldi also does their version. Always have a read of the ingredients when you're out shopping for breakfast cereals. Stay away from any sugar-coated cereals. Even some fruit-containing cereals have a high amount of sugar in there as the dried fruits have been preserved with sugar.

Sometimes breakfast time is a rush, especially when you have young children. In these situations, prepare ahead of time. For example, I blend oats and keep them in a jar. So, when it comes to having porridge or an oats omelette in the morning, they are quick and easy to prepare.

Some good ideas for breakfast for you to try:

- One paratha (without oil or butter) with a good vegetable filling and yogurt
- Porridge with nuts and seed
- Shredded wheat with nuts and seeds
- Wholemeal toast with eggs/beans/avocado/low sugar baked beans, nut butter or seeds
- Idli
- Samo seed kheer
- Wholewheat semiya in milk

Lunch

Our lunch should generally be heavier than our evening meal as we have time to burn off this food for the remainder of the day. If you have Desi food daily, a good idea would be to have it for lunch instead of the evening as it can tend to be heavy. If you have a sandwich on the go, always opt for wholemeal bread or pitta. Pittas are often less processed as they contain less additives so would make a healthier choice. Wraps on the other hand contain multiple additives as they often have a longer best before date. Use a healthy filler for your sandwiches and reduce your intake of processed fillers such as ham or premade sandwich fillers. Instead, prepare your own. If you have leftover meat from the night before, you can add that to your lunch. Have plenty of salad with your lunch, too; we should aim for at least five fruit and vegetables a day, and salad is a great way to help increase our daily intake. We habitually have a packet of crisps with sandwiches, again adding more carbohydrates and fat as they are often fried. Try swapping for carrot sticks or peppers instead. For those looking to eat a lower amount of carbohydrates, swap sandwiches by preparing a salad for lunch instead (see recipe section for idea's).

Those of you who go to work, preparing your lunch beforehand is an excellent idea to prevent you from eating out at lunchtime. As mentioned, you could make extra food the night before, so you have a nice meal for lunch. Try to incorporate a variety of different whole grains into your diet. This way, you receive a range of minerals, vitamins, fibre, and nutrients. These grains are an excellent substitute for wheat and potatoes (check out the recipe section for some ideas). Vegetables are also essential for our diet and are versatile to add to many dishes.

Dinner

Dinner should be kept light as we are less active after our evening meal, especially during winter. Try to have dinner between 6-7 pm to allow you a decent amount of time to digest the food before bedtime. Try to include as many vegetables as possible, such as having a variety of sabzi's and salads and adding lots of vegetables to dishes like pasta, noodles, and rice. Sometimes children are fussy when it comes to vegetables, so you could cook and blend the vegetables to make a sauce for pasta or chicken curry (this way, they have the vegetables without realising). Reduce the carbohydrate intake at night as we are less likely to burn it off. Try simple changes like having a burger with chips but the burger without the bun; that way, you have fewer carbohydrates.

Snacks

For some people who work long hours or drive far distances, snacking is the norm, as it may be a while before they get to have their next meal. In this situation, it's all about choosing a healthy food to snack on. Often, we cut out sugar from our tea but then have a biscuit with it, which can contain far more than the one spoon of sugar we put in our tea. Many snacks we are used to having, such as biscuits, chocolates, and crisps, are often heavily processed with the addition of sugar and bad fats. South Asian snacks such as ghatia, bhujia, and shakarpara are usually fried using refined oils. We can make simple swaps for healthier snacks, such as swapping a packet of crisps for a poppadum instead. The poppadum should be the uncooked ones you can purchase from the Desi shops that can be cooked on the tawa. . Bhujia can be swapped for a palm-sized portion of nuts that have been home-roasted. Here are some healthier snack ideas:

- Hummus and carrots/cucumber/peppers sticks
- Fruits
- Natural yogurt and fruit
- Apple slices with nut butter on top
- Milk
- Homemade lassi
- Nuts (make sure they aren't fried)
- Phool Makhanas (home roasted)
- Panjeeri
- Roasted dal and chana
- Poppadums (cooked on tawa, not fried)

MAKE HEALTHY LIVING A WAY OF LIFE

Type 2 Diabetes disproportionately affects many South Asians. After diagnosis, they often receive medication and are left to navigate their new condition and lifestyle changes with minimal support. This book serves as a guide, educating readers about Diabetes and offering practical advice on preventing and managing the condition within South Asian lifestyles. While cultural-specific diet advice may be lacking in our healthcare systems, this book aims to provide valuable support to South Asian communities.

In the final chapter of this book, we have some lower-carbohydrate recipes for Desi foods for you to try. I have adapted our traditional foods with a healthier twist but all the same beautiful spices. I have left the recipes vegetarian so they can be adapted to include any protein source from soya, paneer, or lentils/beans for vegetarians to chicken, eggs, or fish for those that eat meat.

I hope you have enjoyed reading this book and have gained a better understanding of Diabetes and healthy living.

I wish good health and happiness to all those that have read this book.
Together, I hope one day we can help beat Diabetes.

Stay healthy and happy, and always remember:

Your Health Is In Your Hands

07

RECIPES

Mint & Ajwain Paratha

Cut out the carbohydrates in parathas by swapping the typical aloo paratha for mint and ajwain instead. Mint and ajwain are both powerful herbs for digestion

Ingredients

1 cup wholemeal atta
1 cup of mint leaves
1 tsp ajwain
1 tsp garam masala
¼ tsp salt
1 green chilli

Directions

1. Add the atta, mint, ajwain, garam masala, chilli and salt to a bowl
2. Add water to form a dough and leave to rest for 20 minutes
3. Make parathas on the tawa, to reduce fat content cook without oil or butter

Supergreen Paratha

Using fresh vegetables is a easy way to make parathas more healthy, using broccoli instead of cauliflower makes a lighter paratha. The use of green vegetables helps to boost folic acid levels, provides antioxidants and a range of vitamin's and minerals

Ingredients

1 cup wholemeal atta
Handful of broccoli (washed and grated)
¼ cup spinach (washed and cut small)
1 tsp garam masala
¼ tsp salt
1 green chilli

Directions

1. Add the atta, broccoli, spinach, masala, chilli and salt to a bowl
2. Add water to form a dough and leave to rest for 20 minutes
3. Make parathas on the tawa, to reduce fat content cook without oil or butter

Oaty Omelette

Oats are a great way to start the day. This omelette can be shared on toast or is great and filling on its own. Great way to start the day with slow releasing oats and lots of vegetable

Ingredients

2 tbsp of oats (blended to a fine powder)

Half a pepper (diced into squares)

3-4 mushrooms (washed and diced into squares)

Handful of spinach (cut in small pieces)

1 spring onion

1 tsp garlic Italian seasoning, salt to taste, pinch of pepper

½ teaspoon gram flour

3 tbsp milk

Directions

1. Mix oats, garlic seasoning, salt, pepper and gram flour together in a bowl
2. Add milk to form a thick but runny consistency, can add more milk if needed
3. Add in the vegetables and mix thoroughly
4. Pan fry with 1 tbsp rapeseed oil, then turn and cook the other side. Or alternatively cook the top side in the grill. Cook on medium heat for 10 minutes

Avocado Chutney

Avocados are full of beneficial fats. Fats keep us fuller for longer so having an avocado for breakfast will provide you with good energy release.

Ingredients

1 ripe avocado (peeled and cut, removing the stone)

1 tbsp olive oil

1 green chilli

1 tsp lemon juice

A handful of coriander

Salt to taste

Directions

1. Add all ingredients to a blender and blend until a smooth paste
2. Enjoy on toast, as a side dish, in a wrap or on the side with oven baked pakora's

Mushroom, Spinach, Tomato Toast

This a quick healthy breakfast when paired up with a piece of wholemeal toast

Ingredients

8 cherry tomatoes (cut into halves)
3-4 mushrooms (washed and diced into squares)
½ cup spinach (cut in small pieces)
1 tsp garlic Italian seasoning, salt to taste

Directions

1. In a pan heat 1 tbsp rapeseed oil, then add garlic Italian seasoning
2. Then add tomatoes cook for a minute on medium heat then add mushrooms
3. Once cooked add in the spinach, cook for a further a minute then turn off the gas

Porridge

Oats are beneficial for heart health, adding in cinnamon is a great way to flavour the porridge without adding sugar. Combing this with seeds creates a super nutritious breakfast for slow release energy.

Ingredients

2 tbsp Oats (blended to a fine powder)
½ cup milk
A pinch of cinnamon
Handful of seeds

Directions

1. In a pan add oats and cinnamon and mix in milk
2. Turn on the gas and cook on low heat stirring occasionally so that the oats don't clump
3. Once it comes to the boil, turn off the gas
4. Pour into a bowl and top with seeds

Namkeen Phool Makhane

Also known as Fox Nuts, these are great for a snack at chai time instead of reaching for biscuits or crisps. They are packed with nutrients like calcium & magnesium.

Ingredients

1 cup phul makhane
1 teaspoon ambchuran
1 teaspoon jeera powder
A pinch of Himalayan salt
Squeeze of lemon or lime

Directions

1. Dry roast the makhane until slightly golden
2. Turn off the flame and toss in the lime/lemon, salt, jeera and ambchuran

Panjeeri

Usually consumed during the winter months, this a blend on nuts and seeds. The combination is full of good fats and protein, again making for a healthy snack with Chai. In this recipe we have cut the carbs by not adding atta, sugar and less fat with no ghee.

Ingredients

2 tablespoons sesame seeds
2 tablespoons pumpkin seeds
2 tablespoons melon seeds
2 tablespoons flaxseeds
2 tablespoons raisins
1 handful of almonds
1 handful of cashews
1 handful of pistachios
1 handful of walnuts

Directions

1. Grind all the above ingredients (except raisins)
2. Roast the grinded ingredients in a pan until golden, then add in the raisins
3. Allow to cool and panjeeri is ready to eat

Homemade Healthy Naans

A healthier alternative to shop brought white flour naans, with less carbohydrates and more fibre

Ingredients

1 cup wholemeal chakki atta
1 teaspoon baking powder
½ teaspoon salt
½ cup yogurt
½ teaspoon fresh garlic or powder

Directions

1. Combine the atta, salt, garlic and baking powder
2. Mix the above with the yogurt, adding more or less of the yogurt depending on dough consistency (keep same as you would for making chapatis)
3. Allow to set for at least 30 minutes
4. Heat & cook the first side on the tawa, then flip and cook the other side in the grill

Homemade Pizza

An easy quick recipe for fresh pizzas. With less carbohydrates than regular pizza plus the benefit of wholemeal flour

Ingredients

Same ingredients as above for homemade naans but use half the amount of atta
Vegetables of choice
Tomato puree
Dry oregano
Cheese

Directions

1. Prepare the dough as above and allow to set for 30 minutes
2. Roll out the dough the size of a pizza base
3. Place on a pizza tray and bake in oven at 180°C for 5 mins
4. Take out base and spread on tomato puree. Then Sprinkle with oregano
5. Cover with cheese and add vegetable toppings
6. Bake in oven for 15 minutes at 200°C

Mixed Dal

A great way to get a variety of nutrient's in your diet is to make mixed dal. This simple but delicious recipe is great for a quick meal for the whole family, serve by itself, with a portion of rice or chapati.

Ingredients

½ cup mixed daal

2 tablespoons tomato puree

1 teaspoon jeera, ½ teaspoon garam masala,

¼ teaspoon hing

1 tablespoon grinded ginger

Directions

1. Soak the dal overnight and rinse in cold water the following morning
2. Start tadka - 1 tablespoon rapeseed oil, once warm add in jeera and hing, then add ginger. Then add tomato puree and salt, once it forms a paste add in the dal.
3. Add in 2 cups of water and allow to boil, then simmer on medium flame for 30 minutes until dal is cooked, (add more water as needed) then add in garam masala and fresh coriander

Cajoo Gobi

A twist on aloo gobi, in this dish we've left out the aloo for less carbohydrates. Try to use the whole of the cauliflower including the green leaves as these contain so many nutrients.

Ingredients

1 Cauliflower (use the whole of it including the green leaves

Handful of cashews

1 tbsp jeera powder, 1 tsp haldi, 1 tsp dried methi, 1 tsp amchoor powder, ½ tsp salt

2 tbsp tomato puree

1 tbsp ginger and garlic, 1 green chilli

Directions

1. Cut and wash the cauliflower in small pieces then boil for 10 minutes
2. Drain water from cauliflower and set aside
3. In an over dish add the tomato puree, salt, jeera, haldi, ginger, garlic and chilli
4. Add the cauliflower and cashew to the mixture and combine thoroughly
5. Bake at 180°C for 20 minutes
6. When 5 minutes remain add dried methi, amchoor and garam masala

One Pot Super Greens Saag

Many people avoid making saag as they think it takes too long to cook. For this saag recipe, no oil or butter is needed and its all made in one pot in less than 30 minutes! You can adapt the recipe to use any leafy greens you have at home

Ingredients

1 Broccoli, 1 pack of spinach, 1 pack of kale

1 tbsp garlic, ginger, 1 green chilli

1 tbsp garam masala, ½ tsp salt

Directions

1. Wash and cut the vegetable and put into a large cooking pot
2. Add ginger, garlic, chilli and garam masala, salt
3. Add 1 cup of water, bring to boil then leave to simmer on low heat
4. Once cooked blend together
5. Then leave on low flame and sprinkle in the maize flour a little at a time whilst stirring the mixture until a nice thick consistency is achieved
6. Can be served as is or can add tadka as needed

5 minute Faliya

Green beans contain Vitamin C, Vitamin A, magnesium and calcium. This quick sabzi recipe is perfect for quick evening meal with chapati. We have left out the aloo for less carbohydrates.

Ingredients

Green Beans (faliya)

1 tbsp jeera powder, 1 tsp haldi, 1 tsp amchoor powder, ¼ tsp salt

1 green chilli

Directions

1. Wash and cut the green beans
2. In a pan, heat 1 teaspoon of rapeseed oil, then add in jeera, then haldi, then salt and chilli
3. Add in the green beans and stir to combine the tadka
4. Cook for a few minutes, do not overcook the green beans aim to retain the nice bright green colour

Khichdi

This simple yet comforting food is said to help improve our digestive system especially when feeling low. In this recipe we use just a small amount of rice to help reduce the carbohydrate content of the dish. You can also try swapping the rice for quinoa.

Ingredients

¾ cup mung dal
⅛ cup rice (try to use brown rice) or quinoa
1 tbsp ginger, 1 green chilli
¼ tsp hing, ½ tsp jeera, ½ tsp salt
2 tbsp tomato puree

Directions

1. Soak the dal and rice/quinoa for a few hours beforehand, then wash and rinse & keep aside
2. For tadka use 1 tbsp rapeseed oil, then add jeera then hing, then haldi.
3. Next add ginger and chilli, salt
4. Then add tomato puree, cook until a paste is formed
5. Next add the dal and rice/quinoa and mix in the tadka for a few minutes
6. Add 2 cups of water, bring to boil then leave to simmer on low heat
7. Cook for around 20 minutes, keep checking to see if more water needs to be added

Gajar Mattar

Traditionally this sabzi is usually made using aloo, however in this recipe we have reduced the carbohydrates by avoiding the aloo.

Ingredients

2 carrots
½ cup frozen peas
1 tbsp jeera powder, 1 tsp haldi, ¼ tsp salt
1 green chilli, 1 tbsp ginger and garlic
Fresh coriander (washed and cut)

Directions

1. Wash, peel and dice the carrots in small squares
2. In a pan, heat 1 teaspoon of rapeseed oil, then add in jeera, then haldi, ginger, garlic, chilli, salt and chilli
3. Add in the carrots and peas and stir to combine the tadka
4. Cook for 5- 7 minutes until cooked then add in fresh coriander

Masoori Veg

This makes a great lunch on its own or if you fancy a light dinner with lower carbohydrates. I have used green beans and peas in this recipe, but feel free to use whichever vegetables you have at home

Ingredients

¾ cup split masoor dal

1 tbsp ginger, 1 green chilli

¼ tsp hing, 1 tsp mustard seeds , ½ tsp salt

2 tbsp tomato puree

Any vegetables (diced in squares)

Fresh coriander

Directions

1. Soak the dal for a few hours beforehand, then wash and rinse and keep aside
2. For tadka use 1 tbsp rapeseed oil, then add mustard seeds, heat until they splutter, add then hing
3. Next add ginger and chilli
4. Then add tomato puree and salt cook until a paste is formed
5. Next add the dal and vegetables and mix in the tadka for a few minutes
6. Add 2 cups of water, bring to boil then leave to simmer on low heat
7. Cook for around 20 minutes, keep checking to see if more water needs to be added
8. Once cooked, add in fresh coriander

Baked Baingan

This recipe is a spin off of aloo baingan. Leaving out the potatoes makes a lower carbohydrate sabzi. Aubergines are rich in fibre, calcium and potassium. Cooking them in the oven frees you up to do other things (maybe even quick exercise!).

Ingredients

2 Aubergines

1 tbsp jeera powder, 1 tsp haldi, 1 tsp dried methi,

1 tsp amchoor powder, ½ tsp salt

2 tbsp tomato puree

1 tbsp ginger and garlic, 1 green chilli

1 tsp Lemon juice

1 tbsp rapeseed oil

Directions

1. Wash and cut the aubergines in circles and keep aside
2. In an oven dish add the tomato puree, oil, salt, jeera, haldi, ginger, garlic, chilli, dried methi, amchoor and garam masala.
3. Add the aubergine to the mixture and combine thoroughly.
4. Bake at 180°C for 20 minutes

Baked Wholemeal Veg Loaded Samosa's

Who said samosa's have to be fried, full of aloo and made with white refined flour?! In this twist we use wholemeal chakki atta, we add in lots of vegetables and then we bake them

Ingredients

(For filling)
1 small potato
½ cup peas & sweetcorn
2 carrots (finely diced)
½ cup Spinach finely cut
1 green chilli, ½ tsp salt, 1 tsp jeera,
1 tsp garam masala, ½ tsp ajwain

(For Pastry)
1 cup wholemeal atta
1 tbsp rapeseed oil
¼ tsp salt

Directions

1. First make the dough - in a bowl combine atta, salt and oil and enough water to make a soft dough, then cover and set aside for at least 30 minutes.
2. Next wash and cut the potatoes then boil, once cooked drain well
3. Next start tadka - tbsp rapeseed oil, then add jeera, chilli then peas, carrots, sweetcorn, salt and ajwain, then garam masala. Stop cooking once peas and carrots cooked
4. Next crumble the potatoes into the veg mix, this is our filling complete
5. For the pastry - roll out round thin chapatis then cut in half. Hold the half in hands and make a cone shape to add out filling into
6. Fill the mixture into the cone then press down to seal the edges, repeat this for the rest of the dough until all the mixture is finished
7. Place samosa's onto a baking tray and cook at 180°C for 20 minutes
8. Serve with salad and homemade chutney

Oven Pakora's With Secret Vege's

This is a great quick recipe that you can try for starters for guests. Best part is they are oven cooked and contain lots of nutrient rich vegetables. I even made them for my 11 month old baby (without salt or chilli) and she loved them!

Ingredients

1 small potato
½ cup broccoli
1 carrot
1 onion
1 cup spinach
½ tsp salt
1 tbsp garma masala, 1 tbsp jeera powder, 1tsp dry methi
2 green chilli's
2 tbsp gram flour
1 tbsp yogurt

Directions

1. Wash all vegetables and potato thoroughly then grate the potato, carrot, broccoli
2. Thinly cut onion and spinach and add to the veg mix
3. Then add in methi, jeera, garam masala, chilli, gram flour
4. Add in yogurt (this part gets messy with the hands!) combine well then add salt
5. Line a baking tray with greaseproof paper and brush on a little oil
6. Shape the mixture into small flat shapes, leaving a small gap between each pakora
7. Place samosa's onto a baking tray and cook at 200°C for 20 mins
8. Serve with some lovely homemade chutney

Samo Seeds (Barnyard Millet)

Samo seeds are commonly used during the Navratri fasts. They are lower in carbohydrates and higher in protein and fibre in comparison to rice.

Ingredients

½ cup samo seeds
½ cup peas
1 tbsp ginger, 1 green chilli
½ tsp jeera, ½ tsp salt
2 ripe tomatoes

Directions

1. Wash and rinse the samo seeds then set aside
2. In a pan prepare the tadka, 1 tbsp rapeseed oil, then add jeera, ginger, chilli and salt
3. Next add in peas, once cooked add in samo seeds
4. Then add 2 cups of water, allow to boil then cook on low heat until all the water has been absorbed (usually around 7 minutes)
5. Serve with yoghurt for lunch/dinner or with daal instead of rice accompanied with a nice hearty salad

Cous Cous

Cous Cous is great for salads and a substitute for rice. I normally purchase the wholewheat cous cous from Tesco. Quick and simple to prepare, can be eaten hot or cold.

Ingredients

½ cup cous cous
1 can of chickpeas
1 pepper (any colour) (diced in squares)
½ onion (diced in squares)
½ cup spinach
1 tsp jeera powder, 1 tsp dried oregano, , ¼ tsp salt, ¼ tsp paprika, 1 tsp lemon juice,
1 green chilli, 1 tsp garlic

Directions

1. Soak cous in boiling water (just enough to cover the cous cous) and cover, leave for at least 10 minutes.
2. In a pan prepare tadka, 1tsp rapeseed oil, add onions and peppers, then garlic and chilli and salt.
3. Add in chickpeas, paprika, oregano, and lemon juice, cook for 10 minutes
4. Mix in cous cous and turn of heat

Quinoa Salad

Quinoa is a great grain to add to your diet as its contains all 9 essential amino acids, making a great protein rich food. Quinoa is delicious in a cold salad, warm or even added to homemade burgers.

Ingredients

½ cup Quinoa

¼ cucumber (diced in squares)

1 carrot (grated)

5 small round radishes (cut in small pieces)

1 tbsp extra virgin olive oil

1 tsp balsamic vinegar

Handful of fresh mint leaves (cut finely)

½ tsp Garlic Italian seasoning

Salt to taste

Directions

1. Wash and rinse the quinoa then bring to boil with 1 cup water. Simmer for about 10 minutes until water fully absorbed and seeds open up
2. Sieve the quinoa if any excess water remains and then allow to cool, meanwhile prepare the salad
3. Cut salad as mentioned above, then mix all the ingredient together in a bowl
4. Last step add the quinoa

Cous Cous Salad

This cous cous recipe is a cold salad recipe, perfect for work lunches. Feel free to add in any fruit or salad, also great with pomegranate, meats, soya, cheese, or tuna.

Ingredients

½ cup cous cous

1 can of chickpeas

1 pepper (any colour) (diced in squares)

½ cup spinach

For dressing: 1sp garlic Italian seasoning, 1 tsp lemon juice,

1 tsp olive oil, salt to taste

1 small apple (cut in small squares with skin on)

Directions

1. Soak cous in boiling water (just enough to cover the cous cous) and cover, leave for at least 10 minutes.

1. In a bowl add the remaining ingredients and add in the dressing
2. Final step add in the cous cous

Bulgur wheat

Bulgur wheat is another great grain full of fibre and folate.

Ingredients

½ cup bulgur wheat

½ cup parsley

½ cup tomatoes (chopped into small squares)

½ onion

1tsp lemon juice

½ cup fresh mint

1 tbsp extra virgin olive oil

Directions

1. Wash bulgur wheat then place in a pan to boil. Once boiled, simmer one medium heat for 15 minutes.
2. Drain of the excess water and allow to cool until fully drained (at least 30 minutes)
3. In a bowl add the remaining ingredients, then add the bulgur wheat
4. Mix thoroughly and enjoy as a side dish, with dal or a salad perfect for bbqs

Wholewheat Noodle Stiry Fry

We all love a stir fry, try giving this simple veg loaded noodle stir fry a go. For noodles I use Sainsbury wholewheat noodles. A much healthier option to instant masala noodles, try not to overcook the vegetables, keep them nice and crunchy for maximum nutrients.

Ingredients

1 nest of noodles for 2 people

1 pepper (cut in long strips)

Handful of Sugar snaps or mangetout

Handful of Spinach

Handful of mushrooms

1 carrot (grated)

2 spring onions

1 Tbsp garlic & ginger, 1 chilli, ¼ tsp black pepper and white pepper, 2 tbsp soy sauce, 1tbsp rice vinegar, 1 tsp madras curry powder

Directions

1. In a pan boil the noodles as per pack instructions, then drain and rinse in cold water, set aside
2. In a separate pan, add 1 tbsp of rapeseed oil, ginger, garlic and chilli
3. Then add in all the veg except the spring onion and turn up the heat, stir frequently to prevent the veg burning
4. Then stir in noodles
5. Next add soy sauce, vinegar, pepper, madras curry powder
6. Turn off the gas and sprinkle on spring onion

Veg Loaded Pasta

Pasta is a great quick meal to make, ideal for lunch or dinner. When selecting pasta healthier options are wholemeal, chickpea, pea, or lentil pastas as they have a low GI, meaning they will keep us fuller for longer as they release glucose slowly.

Ingredients

1 cup pasta (as above)
I cup Tomato puree
Courgette (chopped in small pieces)
½ cup sweetcorn
½ cup spinach
½ onion (diced)
1 pepper (diced)
5-6 mushrooms (chopped in chunks)
1tsp dried oregano, 1tsp basil, ¼ tsp pepper, ¼ tsp salt, 1tsp garlic, 1 fresh chilli

Directions

1. Boil pasta as per pack instruction
2. In a separate pan prepare the sauce, add 1tsp rapeseed oil then add onion, peppers, garlic and salt
3. Then add in courgettes, sweetcorn and mushroom, once cooked add herbs
4. Mix the pasta into the sauce, then plate up. Can add cheese if like and serve with a nice salad

Apple Chutney

Many premade chutneys often contain sugar. With this recipe you can use any fruit you have at home, great alternative are peaches, pineapple and mangoes and you don't need to add any sugar as there is natural sweetness from the fruits.

Ingredients

1 apple (cut in in large pieces but leave on the skin)
½ cup fresh mint leaves (thoroughly washed)
½ cup fresh coriander (thoroughly washed)
A few grapes
½ onion
1 green chilli
1tsp amchoor, ¼ tsp salt, 1 tsp jeera powder

Directions

1. Add all ingredients to pestle and mortar (moosal and oukhli) and grind together or blend together in a blender. Can add a little water if needed.

Lassi

This recipe for salted lassi is a great source of protein, calcium, B12 and packed with probiotics, best part is it takes less than 5 minutes to prepare

Ingredients

1 cup yogurt
1 cup of water
1 tsp grinded roasted jeera
Salt to taste
Optional - pinch of kala namak

Directions

1. On a tawa heat the jeera seeds until roasted. Then grind the seed to a powder
2. In a jug add the yogurt and water and using a hand whisk, mix together
3. Add in the jeera, salt and kala namak
4. Lassi is ready

Fruity Yogurt

Many fruity yogurts from the supermarkets either contain added sugar, sweetener's or artificial flavours. Preparing your own is so quick, easy and healthy. Simply add any fruit into natural yogurt, great for dessert or as a snack and a healthier choice for kids too.

Ingredients

1 bowl of natural yogurt
Fruit of choice cut into small pieces

Directions

1. Cut the fruit into small pieces and combine into the yogurt and enjoy

Chaat

A great alternative starter to fried foods. If you don't have these fruits to hand, feel free to use any fruit you have at home

Ingredients

1 potato (cut in small squares and boiled)
1 apple grated
1 grated carrot
Pomegranate seeds
1 can of chickpeas (washed & drains)
½ tsp chaat masala
½ onion
½ cup yogurt
Homemade chutney
1 tsp grinded roasted jeera
1 green chilli
Fresh imli (tamarind)

Directions

1. In individual bowls add the potato, top with a few spoons of yogurt
2. Then sprinkle on some of the apple, carrot, chickpeas, onion, pomegranate
3. On top add jeera, chaat masala, chilli and mix thoroughly
4. Sprinkle imli and chutney on top

Beetroot Burgers

We often rely on shop brought processed burgers, but vegetable burgers are so easy to make. This recipe can be adapted to any vegetables or beans that you have at home. Beetroots are great for the immune system, packed with vitamins and full of fibre.

Ingredients

1 beetroot (peeled and grated)
1 carrot (peeled and grated)
1 can of red kidney beans
1tsp garlic, 1tsp oregano, 1 tsp jeera, ¼ tsp salt,1 green chilli
1 tsp lemon or lime juice
1 tbsp cornflour/arrowroot/rice flour/chickpea flour

Directions

1. In a bowl add the beetroot, carrot, kidney beans and mash by hand or use a masher
2. Next add the seasoning and lemon juice and mix well
3. Add cornflour and combine well then set aside for 20 minutes
4. Shape the mixture into burgers and either pan fry with 1 tablespoon rapeseed oil or bake in oven for 20 minutes at 180°C

Hummus

This simple recipe is great as a sandwich filler, as a side dish or as a snack with carrot, cucumbers or peppers

Ingredients

1 can of chickpeas (washed & drained)
1 garlic clove
¼ tsp salt
1tbsp tahini paste
1tbsp olive oil
4 tbsp water

Directions

1. Add all the above ingredients to a blender and blend until a smooth paste
2. Serve in a bowl and enjoy

Red Lentil Tofu

Tofu is often made by processing soy beans. Try this simple homemade fresh recipe of Tofu made from red lentils instead. A great Tofu to add to salads or mains for extra protein.

Ingredients

1 cup of split masoor dal
Water
¼ tsp salt
Semolina (sooji)
1tbsp of rapeseed oil
1tsp Garlic powder or granules
1tbsp Jeera powder

Directions

1. Soak the dal in water for at least 4 hours
2. Wash the dal thoroughly and then soak in boiling water (2 cups water)
3. Once cooled add the dal and water to a blender and blend until a smooth paste
4. Add the blended dal to a saucepan and add the salt and jeera powder and heat on low heat for 10-15 minutes and continue whisking to prevent any clumps forming. It should start to thicken up
5. Next pour the dal into a deep dish and allow to set. Once cool place into the fridge and leave for at least 4 hours
6. Take out of the fridge and cut into small squares
7. In a separate bowl, mix a tablespoon of sooji and the garlic powder and a pinch of salt
8. Spread the dal squares onto a oven dish and mix in the oil and then the sooji mix
9. Cook in the oven for 20 minutes at 200°C

The
Desi Diabetes
Guide

Useful Resources

Websites:

desidiabetes.co.uk
diabetes.co.uk
diabetes.org.uk
nhs.uk
fareehajay.com
myfitnesspal.com

Instagram:

@desidiabetes

YouTube:

@desidiabetesuk
@lucywyndhamread (7 minute exercise videos)

Books:

Carbs & Cals - World Foods - Cheyette C & Balolia Y
Carbs & Cals - Carbs & Calorie Counter - Cheyette C & Balolia Y
The Doctors Kitchen - Dr Rupy Aujla
Yog Sadhana And Yoga Healing Secrets - Swami Ramdev

References

1 - Diabetes.co.uk 2019, Diabetes In South Asians, accessed: 25 February 2023 (https://www.diabetes.co.uk/south-asian/)

2 - World Health Organization, 2023, Diabetes, accessed 14 November 2022, (Diabetes (who.int))

3 - NICE, Clinical Knowledge Summaries, 2023 Diabetes - type 2:When should I suspect type 2 diabetes in an adult?, accessed 12 December 2022, (Diagnosis in adults | Diagnosis | Diabetes - type 2 | CKS | NICE)

4 - Diabetes.co.uk, 2022 , Pre Diabetes (Borderline Diabetes), accessed 11 November 2022, (Prediabetes or Borderline Diabetes)

5 - GP Notebook 2020, Diabetes in remission, accessed 12 December 2022, diabetes in remission - General Practice notebook (gpnotebook.com)

6 - NICE, 2022, Type 2 diabetes in adults: management, accessed 11 November 2022, (Recommendations | Type 2 diabetes in adults: management | Guidance | NICE)

7 - NHS 2022, Cholesterol Levels, High Cholesterol, accessed 12 December 2022, (High cholesterol - Cholesterol levels - NHS (www.nhs.uk))

8 - NICE, 2023 Cardiovascular disease: risk assessment and reduction, including lipid modification, Clinical guideline [CG181], 5 June 2023, (Recommendations | Cardiovascular disease: risk assessment and reduction, including lipid modification | Guidance | NICE)

9 - NICE, 2019, Hypertension in adults: diagnosis and treatment, accessed 1 July 2023, (NG136 Visual summary (nice.org.uk))

10 - Diabetes UK, having a hypo, accessed 1 July 2023, (Having a hypo | Guide to diabetes | Diabetes UK)

11 - GOV.UK, Diabetes and driving, accessed 22 July 2023, (Diabetes and driving - GOV.UK (www.gov.uk))

12 - NICE, 2023, Type 2 diabetes in adults, Quality standard [QS209], accessed 1 July 2023, (Quality statement 6: 9 key care processes | Type 2 diabetes in adults | Quality standards | NICE)

13 - University of Dundee, 2022 South Asians predisposed to type 2 diabetes at younger age, accessed 5 June 2023, (South Asians predisposed to type 2 diabetes at younger age | University of Dundee)

14 - Diabetes UK, risk of type 2 diabetes in the south asian community, accessed 1 July 2023, (Risk of Type 2 diabetes in the South Asian community | Diabetes UK)

15 - Diabetes.co.uk, 2022, Diabetes and Obesity, accessed 5 June 2023, (Diabetes and Obesity)

16 - GOV.UK, 2020, GuidanceHealth matters: physical activity - prevention and management of long-term conditions, accessed 1 July, 2023, (Health matters: physical activity - prevention and management of long-term conditions - GOV.UK (www.gov.uk))

17 - Swami Ramdev, 2005, Yog Sadhana And Yoga Healing Secrets, 1st edition, Divya Prakashan, Uttaranchal

18 - food sugar averages as per individual packages

19 - Mehar S, Dr John J S, Cheyette C, Balolia Y, 2019, Carbs & Cals, World Foods, Chello Publishing, Great Britain

20 - Drinkaware, 2023, What is an alcohol unit?, accessed 5 June 2023, (What is an alcohol unit? | Drinkaware)

21 - Food Standards Agency, 2020, Check The Label, accessed 1 July 2023, (Check the label | Food Standards Agency)

22 - British Heart Foundation, Food Portions, Accessed 5 June 2023 (Food portions - Heart Matters magazine - BHF)

23 - Fareeha Jay, Accessed 24 July 2023, (https://www.fareehajay.com/)

24 - World Health Organisation, 2023, Aspartame hazard and risk assessment results released, accessed 14 July 2023, Aspartame hazard and risk assessment results released (who.int)

25 - Diabetes.co.uk, 2019, Fenugreek & Diabetes, accessed 20 July 2023, Fenugreek - Blood Sugar Levels Effects & Metabolism (diabetes.co.uk)

26 Diabetes.co.uk, 2019, Bitter Melon & Diabetes, accessed 20 July 2023, Bitter Melon - Effect on Blood Glucose Levels & Benefits (diabetes.co.uk)

27 - The Times, 2023, Poor Diet & Lifestyle Blamed For Soaring Diabetes in India, accessed 14 July 2023, (Poor diet and lifestyle blamed for soaring diabetes in India (thetimes.co.uk)

28 - Diabetes UK, risk of type 2 diabetes in the south asian community, accessed 20 July 2023, (Risk of Type 2 diabetes in the South Asian community | Diabetes UK)

29 - Cheyette C & Balolia Y, 2016, Carbs & Cals, Carbs & Calorie Counter, 6th edition, Chello Publishing, Great Britain

30 - My Fitnesspal

31 - Sporting Equals, 2018, Research Report into South Asian Women and Inactivity, accessed 1 June 2023, (South Asian Women and Inactivity Executive Summary Report Dec 2018.pdf (sportingequals.org.uk)

32 - Diabetes.co.uk, 2023, Diabetes Life Expectancy, accessed 31/5/24, (https://www.diabetes.co.uk/diabetes-life-expectancy.html)

33 - Mackintosh, J.E. et al. (2020) 'Potential prevention of diabetes and obesity by achieving macronutrient balance: a guide for diet and fast food,' the British Journal of Diabetes, 20(1), pp. 61–69. https://doi.org/10.15277/bjd.2020.245.

The Desi Diabetes Guide

@desidiabetes

desidiabetesuk

desidiabetes.co.uk

Printed in Great Britain
by Amazon

51806945R00064